The Imagineering Workout

Exercises to Shape Your Creative Muscles

Compiled and Edited by Peggy Van Pelt

EDITIONS

LOS ANGELES NEW YORK

By the Disney Imagineers
Compiled and Edited by Peggy Van Pelt

A Camphor Tree Book
Design and layout by Bruce Gordon
Sketches of Figment created by Larry Nikolai

Disney Editions
Wendy Lefkon, Editorial Director
Jody Revenson, Editor

For information address Disney Editions
1101 Flower Street, Glendale, California 91201.

Printed in the United States of America

First edition, 2005

10 9 8

Library of Congress Cataloging-in-Publication Data on file.

ISBN 0-7868-5554-1
FAC-025438-15345

SUSTAINABLE FORESTRY INITIATIVE

Certified Chain of Custody
Promoting Sustainable Forestry

www.sfiprogram.org
SFI-01054

The SFI label applies to the text stock.

Table of Contents

Why This Book?

Jody Revenson
Editor, Disney Editions

*If we go to a gym to shape and tone our bodies with physical
exercises, then why aren't we doing creative exercises
to shape and tone our imaginations?*

Since most Imagineering projects start with story, here's mine: I returned from a magical cruise with a garishly painted papier-mâché sea horse to complement the "Under the Sea" decor in the "smallest room" in my home. I intended to hang it in a corner but discovered that my ceilings were made of tissue paper and could not hold a hook. I stood there like a schlub, staring at the walls (and the several holes in the ceiling) and fumed. There *had* to be a way to accomplish this. I thought, who does stuff like this? Maybe I could learn from their example. And it occurred to me that I have the privilege of knowing *exactly* those kinds of people, people who accomplish creative acts of engineering every day. So I asked myself—what would an Imagineer do?

Having read *The Imagineering Way*, our previous publication about the essence of the Imagineering culture, my first thought was, this is *possible*. Then I asked myself about what I wanted as the end result. I pictured the room with the sea horse hanging in the corner. And then I thought, what am I thinking? I'm no Imagineer. Which led to a thought about lunch and doing laundry and giving up entirely.

I took a deep breath and forced myself to try again. How could I suspend it in the air? What tools do I have to do this or where could I go to get them? It took me a little while (and a few more holes in the walls) but I figured a way to hang it by stringing it between the two corner walls using, ironically, fishing line.

While hanging a papier-mâché sea horse, coming up with a new recipe to feed the family, or even putting together a presentation for a new client may not typically be thought of as creative acts, they are. Creativity is about choices, training, experimentation, inspiration, history, commitment, and fun. Every occupation—from artist to businessperson, teacher to chef—requires us to imagine, create, and execute ideas. No matter what you're doing, you're being creative.

Most of us have to work out daily, weekly, or at the least, before the high school reunion, to get and keep our bodies in shape. So why aren't we doing the same for our *creative* muscles?

The best part of this kind of exercising is that you don't need to buy gym clothes; you don't get too sweaty (unless you want to); and you can do it anywhere and everywhere. The equipment isn't cumbersome or costly, often just a pen, scissors, paper, and time. You can devise your own workout program based on your current needs ("fitting" into that upcoming presentation) or potential opportunities (deciding to redecorate the entire house).

I couldn't think of a better group of "personal trainers" than the Imagineers, who deal with creative challenges on a daily basis. After working with them for a while, I noticed how I had been trying to "think like an Imagineer" when I needed to accomplish not only creative but also practical endeavors. That's how I came up with the idea for this book. I no longer wanted to "imagine" how an Imagineer thought. I wanted to develop the skills they had, using their own methods.

Just like the human body, creativity has its own diversity of muscle groups, and here you will find a wide assortment of exercises that addresses each in its own way. At first read, some exercises might seem similar, but in actuality they are truly distinctive adaptations which demonstrate a variety of approaches. Coming from such a highly diverse group of people, these similar ideas have been adapted to each individual's unique experience, training, educational focus, and thinking and communication style. Some exercises tackle a specific target; others offer a broader point of view, which can be applied to a variety of situations. Some might seem to have nothing to do with your needs, but even an awareness of the process may provide inspiration when an unexpected opportunity comes your way.

Tackling any new enterprise can be daunting, but once you have worked out your creative muscles, you will know anything is possible—even when you want to hang a papier-mâché sea horse from a tissue-paper ceiling.

Seeking Creative Balance

How to Use This Book

Peggy

Peggy Van Pelt
Author, Artist, and Editor of *The Imagineering Workout*

There are as many ways to use a book on creativity as there are creative people who will read it!

The Imagineering Workout is designed for those who are interested in shaping and toning their creative muscles. It's written from the collective practice, wit, and wisdom of over one hundred Imagineers—each creative and yet each different in their creative expression. As a result, this book is a collection of exercises, note cards, write-in cards, jotted notes, journal pages, and illustrations that capture aspects of the creative process and routines Imagineers use daily to keep their creative muscles in the best of condition.

How you use this book is really up to you! If you're beginning to explore your creativity, you might consider the first sections on getting started and warming up before moving on to the others. If you're well into developing your creativity, approach the book as you would a creative project and dig right in. Either way, it is important that you make any exercise you do your own. Twist it, spin it, or rewrite it to suit your special talents, abilities, or skills (Imagineers do that without reservation!). Remember, it's all about stretching your creative muscles.

Record your experiences, experiments, and results directly in the book, if you want to. Fold over page corners, underline text, or visually mark favorite exercises, words of wisdom, and illustrations. Try the unfamiliar—especially those things that you're sure won't work or you don't like. If something doesn't work for you, keep changing it until it does. Question everything with positive curiosity. Let your imagination work for you—it wants to be directed by your interests and passion.

Make this *your* book. Draw inspiration from it to heighten creative achievements and boldly re-write it to suit your creative needs. Your objective is to condition your creative muscles to respond on demand.

You are allowed to draw or write in this book, wherever you want!

You have permission to color outside the lines!

Imagineering Exercises . . .

Chris Runco

"Yes, If . . ."

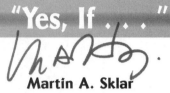

Martin A. Sklar

Vice Chairman and Principal Creative Executive, Walt Disney Imagineering

It seems as though every week, there's a new book out about how to be creative.

I must admit I don't read them. Why? Because I suspect most of them are full of theories and not based on actual performance.

My fellow Disney Legend, Bob Gurr (who designed the original Disneyland Monorail, Autopia cars, and Main Street vehicles) had his own axiom for creative challenges: "Practice always works because it knows no theory." I'm sure he was listening to our boss, Walt Disney, when Walt said, "The way to get started is to stop talking and start doing!"

Walt Disney was the eternal optimist. He believed in the future—that the world could be a better place if only we focused on people's needs and applied the best ideas of science and technology and creative imagination to challenges old and new. And if we were willing to "take a chance" on our new solutions . . . recognizing that failure was a possible consequence of stepping out from the norm.

My friend Harrison (Buzz) Price, whose economic feasibility and site-location studies fueled the development of Disneyland and Walt Disney World, postulated the "Yes, if . . . " method of analyzing projects and reporting his findings to Walt Disney. "'Yes, if . . . ' is the language of an enabler," Buzz wrote in his book *Walt's Revolution! By the Numbers* (Ripley Entertainment, Inc., 2003). "It pointed to what needed to be done to make the possible plausible. Walt liked this language. 'No, because' is the language of a deal killer. 'Yes, if . . . ' is the approach of a deal maker. Creative people thrive on 'Yes, if . . . '"

When I enter my office each day, one of the first things I see is this quote from Walt Disney: "Somehow I can't believe that there are many heights that can't be scaled by a man who knows the secret of making dreams come true. This special secret can be summarized in four Cs. They are Curiosity, Confidence, Courage, and Constancy, and the greatest of these is Confidence. When you believe a thing, believe in it all the way. Have confidence in your ability to do it right. And work hard to do the best possible job."

As Imagineers, we are used to facing new challenges every day, and focusing on the next blank sheet of paper as a brand-new opportunity to let our imaginations loose. We love to explore and try new things. We try to remember Walt Disney's four Cs as we develop new projects for Disney Parks and Resorts from California to Florida, from Paris to Tokyo, and now for Hong Kong, as well as at sea for the Disney Cruise Line. And we love to share Walt Disney's vision for getting started: "Stop talking and start doing!"

There is no major formula, but we think *The Imagineering Workout* can offer ideas for practical (and sometimes ingenious) exercises that will help you get started on your next creative adventure. We hope we stimulate your thinking, encourage ideas, and inspire new approaches.

Will these approaches help you and others who use this workbook think "out of the box?" I believe they will, because creative people create their own boxes . . . and learn to work inside and outside any box they are given. And creative people thrive on "Yes, if . . . !"

Scaling that Blank Sheet of Paper

Storytelling, Storyboarding

Tom Fitzgerald
Executive Vice President, Senior Creative Executive

What is the origin of storytelling?

Storytelling is probably the oldest form of communication. In fact, it's been around so long that John Hench, Disney Legend and Senior Vice President of Creative Development used to insist that it's "in our genes." Storytelling has played a vital role in our survival . . . allowing us to share information, knowledge, and values from generation to generation. Story is the medium through which we receive our early learning as to right and wrong, good versus evil, reward and punishment, social values, etc. Whether genetically based or learned, we respond to storytelling. It engages our attention and no matter how old we get, who doesn't love a good story? Storytelling works!

What is the function of the storyboard?

Walt Disney invented the storyboard in the days of his early cartoon films. Basically, storyboards are a series of images that illustrate the flow and continuity of a story. It's a tool that allowed Walt Disney and his artists to envision a film prior to production. And it allowed Walt's team to have a shared vision of the story they were telling and how it would unfold. In addition to driving the creative development, storyboards offered Walt a cost-effective way to experiment with a film prior to cameras rolling.

When Walt ventured into live-action films, he continued to use storyboards to pre-visualize the story. At Walt Disney Imagineering, we carry on the tradition, often storyboarding rides, shows, and films for our theme parks around the world. Starting in brainstorming sessions with note cards, quick sketches, and plenty of push pins, we capture our first thoughts, ideas, images, and feelings about the story we are creating. We work and re-work the boards until we feel that our story is strong and clear. Only then do we venture onto a soundstage or proceed with models and three-dimensional production.

At Walt Disney Imagineering, everything we do revolves around the story, and storyboards are an essential tool in helping us tell the story. So often it all starts with images or words recorded on note cards pinned to a wall. The note cards are a recurring motif that you will find as you venture forth discovering your own creative ideas and the stories you want to tell.

Dream and Do!

Kevin Rafferty
Senior Concept Writer-Director

Tackling creative challenges head-on is the heart and soul of Walt Disney Imagineering.

Since 1952, Imagineers have been turning impossible dreams and schemes into magical rides, shows, and attractions for Disney theme parks around the world. Everything we do begins with that small, but powerful, spark of an idea. As soon as that spark ignites and we begin to ask ourselves, "what if . . . ?"—watch out!

Anyone can dream. But Imagineers dream and do. And so can you! If you can face your creative challenge with passion and positive thinking, amazing things will happen. Amazing things happen around Imagineering every day because we don't sit around and simply ponder the possibilities (or impossibilities). We roll up our sleeves and get to work!

Our way of working is fueled by our desire to tell a multidimensional story. Once we create a strong theme or story, we use it as a "design hook" upon which we can hang our entire design. When an idea is in development, everything we do is informed by the story. For example, a non-Disney ride engineer designs a vehicle for a basic free-fall—type ride system. But an Imagineering ride engineer designs a creaky old service elevator for a haunted Hollywood hotel, circa 1939. It's all about making the ordinary extraordinary!

Can a theme and/or story help your idea? Let's say you want to create a special party. You begin by going to the party store and picking up the usual favors and decorations, right? Wrong! Try turning your thinking around. For example, how about giving your party an underwater theme? With that theme in mind, can you imagine all the possibilities? You can dive in headfirst to your party planning because everything you do now will be informed by that undersea theme. Many of your ideas can be brought to life with the help of a strong theme or story to guide you along.

Our story began when Walt Disney asked his filmmakers to expand upon what they already knew about storytelling and movie making in order to help him invent the theme park industry. He had the uncanny ability to recognize creative talents in someone that they, themselves, didn't know they had. For instance, Walt had seen special effects animator Blaine Gibson's sculpture exhibited at the Studio library on several occasions. After Blaine worked with Marc Davis on Pirates of the Caribbean for Disneyland, Walt asked Blaine to become Imagineering's lead sculptor. Blaine went on to sculpt every ghost, pirate, and president you've ever seen in a Disney theme park. Walt recognized the story potential in studio artist X. Atencio and asked him to come to Imagineering to become the show writer for a new idea he was thinking about called Pirates of the Caribbean. Atencio, who had never written anything professionally in his life, much less song lyrics, wrote "Yo Ho, Yo Ho (A Pirate's Life for Me)."

These are only a few of the countless stories about Imagineers who didn't realize what they were capable of until they started doing it. When author Ray Bradbury came to speak at Imagineering one day, someone asked, "What do you have to do to become a writer?" Ray responded, "Write, write, write!" You can sit around and think about your idea or creative project all day long, but it will never happen if you let your fear of taking the first practical step get the best of you. Rather, let your project get the best of you!

Imagineers try and fail and keep trying until they make magic. Our ideas are often so unusual and one-of-a-kind that we don't always know what we're doing or where we're going until we get started. But we get started. And that's the key.

Isn't it time you got started?

Go ahead. Tackle that creative challenge head-on. Allow that spark of an idea to ignite your creativity and passion. Whatever your dream or scheme; whether it be creating a themed party, writing a poem, or sculpting for the first time, to make that dream come true, don't just sit there—dream and do!

ONE LITTLE SPARK
OF INSPIRATION
CARRIES US TO NEW
HEIGHTS OF CREATIVITY!

Your Creative License

Bernie

Bernie Mosher
Director, Creative Development Services, Walt Disney Imagineering Florida

In 1990, I was living in France, working as the Project Engineer on Frontierland for Disneyland Paris. My project teammate, Barbara Wightman, was our interior designer, and she is the originator of this creative license.

While working with Barbara, I would often remark to her how talented and creative I thought she was. Barbara would reciprocate by telling me that I was also creative; but I would rebuff the compliment by saying, "I'm an engineer, not a creative person like you." One day during such an exchange, Barbara stopped, picked up a piece of paper and wrote on it: *You are Creative.* She completed the declaration by drawing a seal on the paper, making it official.

This simple act reminded me that we each express ourselves in different ways. Engineering and problem solving require both an imagination and an ability to think beyond obstacles and limits. I kept my creative license as a reminder that creativity is not limited to fine arts such as painting, music, or literature; creativity is a part of us all.

When we were brainstorming ideas for *The Imagineering Workout*, I related this story and how much Barbara's creative license had meant to me. The group liked the idea of a license for the book, and with the help of graphic designers Andre Greppi and Jeff Morris, we created one, using Barbara's as inspiration.

Now it's your turn—fill in the license and make your creativity official, too!

*Creative License design by
Andre Greppi, Visual Arts Specialist III, and
Jeff Morris, Graphic Designer Sr. Principal,
Walt Disney Imagineering Florida*

LICENSE

THIS CERTIFIES THAT

_____

IS RECOGNIZED

AS A CREATIVE INDIVIDUAL WHO POSSESSES
THE QUALITY AND ABILITY TO THINK CREATIVELY
AND PROBLEM-SOLVE IN INNOVATIVE AND UNIQUE WAYS.

_____
Date

**THIS IS YOUR LICENSE TO BE
AS CREATIVE AS YOU WOULD LIKE
WITH NO LIMITATIONS!**

Warming Up

Art is not devoid of reason or intellect. It's packed with it. It's just not driven by it. How can I put this? Maybe it's that the artist is like a train riding on the tracks of experience and logic, but the steam which drives him or her is emotion and vision.

—Steve Cook
Senior Staff Assistant
Creative Development

When it comes to your creative ability, don't worry if your glass is half full or half empty . . . just knock it over and use every last drop.

—Jason Grandt
Graphic Designer
Creative Development

I look at the art that surrounds me in my office and seek inspiration. I reflect on the work of my heroes and think to myself, "What would Van Gogh, Klimt, Warhol, or Tamayo do?

—Leticia G. Lelevier
Senior Show Producer
Creative Development

Talent

Dan Dillon
Principal Graphic Designer, Walt Disney Imagineering Florida

Ever feel creativity is an illusive dream that only the few can grasp? Everyone is talented—it's natural to us!

The reality is that everyone is talented. It's evident in things such as learning language as a child. This is a creative tool from the first words we speak to mastering the art of storytelling and communication. Or, how about that first crayon wall mural? It was an absolute work of art—wasn't it? Although it probably looked much like a psychedelic hairball, it was nonetheless evidence of emerging ability.

Talent isn't just the ability to paint a portrait, compose a symphony, or sculpt a statue—it's about the possible. A creative mind is always working. Where it expresses it is your choice.

> **Try this simple exercise:**
>
> **Get a pencil and a napkin or a 3 x 5 card.**
>
> **Draw a box, a simple window you can look through.**
>
> **Above the window, write in bold letters "IMPOSSIBLE."**
>
> **Erase the "IM."**

Look through the window you sketched and let your mind go through it.

A new world's waiting for your creative mind and talents. Now, make a choice. Focus on the abilities that come naturally to you and make things possible. Now you have no excuses. Get rid of what's been holding you back.

Talent is within you. Enjoy letting it out.

Inspiration

John Kavelin
Director, Design & Production, Tokyo Disneyland Resort

Inspiration comes from things that are infused with life.

The word *inspire* means "to breathe into or upon; to infuse with life by breathing." When we say, "I am inspired," it has a deeper significance than we think. We are "breathing in" the living environment of ideas, enthusiasm, and energy that comes with the creative process.

In creating, we are always working from a basis of our training, exposure to others' work, our research, and our life experience. Working together, we can be inspired by our collective histories, training, experience, our predecessors, and our mentors. In my work, I call upon the support of artists and others whose creativity has had a powerful influence on me. These are people from history whose work has transcended time.

> **Select your creative challenge. It can be painting, inventing, or writing. Then, make a list of those creative souls who could inspire a solution, such as Georgia O'Keeffe, Albert Einstein, or Ernest Hemingway. Select one or more people from the list, reflect on their unique talent, research their work, let them breathe life into your thinking and imagination. Now, find your own answers by letting your imagination play with multiple solutions.**

I used this process on a thorny creative problem when called to design a huge stage set and audience seating arrangement for the Jacob Javits Convention Center in New York. After nineteen different solutions, I was still hitting a wall. My sister suggested that I ask for inspiration from someone I admire. I thought about all those whose creativity, style, and originality had withstood the test of time who could help work out this complex design, and the architect Frank Lloyd Wright came to mind. I reflected on his unique talent during a dedicated period of meditation, and then researched his body of work. Within a few days I had a totally new and highly successful solution to my design problem.

When we are inspired, ideas that are living inside us
will find a way to be expressed.

Passion

Michael G. Kennedy
Senior Show Designer, Walt Disney Imagineering Florida

*If you are moved by music or photographs, or if you are swept
away by a dance, you've glimpsed a key to unlocking your
deeper creative convictions . . . passion.*

Answer yes or no to the questions below for insights into your passions and creative inclinations.

Art and Photography

Do you feel strong emotions when creating your own work or viewing others'?
Do images stay with you as memorable?
Do you want to capture or recreate images you've seen?

Music

Are you moved when you hear a favorite piece of music?
Do these feelings stir or instill a vision in you?
Do you feel music is a worthwhile human endeavor?

Dance

Do you enjoy dancing or watching dance?
Do you feel your body is capable of free physical expression?
Are you aware of your own body language?

Food

Do you enjoy the taste of food?
Do you enjoy cooking and experimenting with tastes and textures?
Do certain aromas sweep your mind back to past times and celebrations?

Writing

Do you write letters to those you care about or to yourself (a diary or journal)?
Do you enjoy reading?
Have you ever memorized a poem or literary passage for personal reasons?

Decorating

Does a lavish visual display inspire you?

Would you love to do more decorating in your own surroundings?

Do you feel a deep sense of accomplishment when trimming your house for a holiday?

Design and Craftsmanship

Do you value or create handcrafted things?

Does the touch and feel of hand-wrought items connect you to your childhood?

Do you feel a special connection to architecture or a piece of furniture?

If you answered yes to any one of these questions, you have a creative passion! Let that spirit out and—this is crucial—let it find you. It will come in a compelling moment. You'll feel a need, a true desire to express yourself creatively.

Goals

Dave Crawford

Principal Mechanical Engineer, Show/Ride Engineering

*Setting goals before and during the creative process
enhances your project results.*

It is important to make sure your goal and any up-front assumptions of how to get to that goal are realistic. Answering the following questions will help you create and set a direction for your goals.

> **What are the absolute bottom line requirements for the project?**
> **What are the up-front assumptions of how to meet the goal or
> set the direction? Are they correct?**
> **What short- and long-term goals need to be established?**
> **Who needs to know the goals?**
> **What questions need to be asked?**
> **Is there a way to clarify or revise the goals at any time?**
> **What can you learn from setting goals?**

I learned the importance of this exercise on a project for developing a simple motion-base platform for a virtual-reality-based 3-D video game. Our requirement was to use the main actuators to shake the platform at a very high frequency. In asking about the project goal, I discovered that the designers wanted the actuators to vibrate the floor of the motion base to make it feel as though a huge snake was sliding under the floorboards, scraping the boards with its scales. This revised the goal from "Install high frequency response actuators" to "Make it feel as though a snake is sliding under the floor," opening up a whole range of realistic cost- and time-effective options.

*Goals help you stay on track. Short- and long-term goals work
together, assisting you to know where the project is to go
(desired end result) and how it will get there. The key is to make
sure the goals inspire and don't detract from your
creative journey.*

Long- and short-term thinking both have their place in planning a creative project. Long-term thinking creates the foundation for the future by providing for growth expansion. But you need to establish short-term goals and objectives as a strategy to propel the process toward the long-term creative vision.

—Wing Chao
Executive Vice President
Master Planning, Architecture and Design

There is nothing in a caterpillar that tells you it's going to be a butterfly.

—Buckminster Fuller

Getting Started

*Never paint anything until at least a
year after you have seen it.*

—an old Chinese saying

Adults who remain curious have learned to "not care" about what others think or they had enough confidence as children to keep their curiosity.

—Katie Roser
Prop/Set Designer
Walt Disney Imagineering Florida

Creative refers to every single aspect of life, not only what you do, but how you do it, and how you think about the world.

—Mk Haley
Technology Resources Manager
Image and Effects

What's the central issue for individual designers? Choose your actions! Will I think or not, create or not, work or not, fight or not, or be intimidated? Where's the "Will I" meter today?

—Paul Kay Comstock
Director of Landscape Design
Landscape Architecture

Success is measured by what it means to you. Keep your challenges achievable by using your standards for success. Define what success means to you and the project. Does the definition support your challenges and help you achieve your goals?

—Dave Minichiello
Principal Concept Designer
Walt Disney Imagineering Florida

The Secret to a Successful Start

Jason Surrell
Show Writer, Walt Disney Imagineering Florida

Even Mary Poppins said, "A job begun is half done."

Whatever you hope to accomplish, from sorting the laundry to adding on to your house to starting the great American novel (or more likely the great American screenplay these days), just dive in and "start doing," as Walt Disney said. Sometimes it's important to start doing even before you have a chance to start thinking.

You don't have to like what you're producing—the good news is, you're already over the hurdle of starting and into the process.

> Ball up that first pair of socks from the laundry, make that first hole in the wall for the new den, or type the first sentence of that masterpiece. Once you start, the creative juices begin to flow whether you're aware of it or not, and it's only a matter of time before you're doing your best work and the task is finished.

Mountains of ideas—ideas of mountains

It's not about doing it perfectly from the start; it's about getting started and then improving it.

Start Anywhere

Neil Engel

Senior Principal Production Show Designer, Creative Development

In order to get started, think of something that interests you.

Close your eyes and imagine: exotic fish, roller coasters, rock formations, the origin of the universe, historical events, heroes, scary things. Then choose one.

Zoom in: look closely at your choice. Have a "what if" conversation with yourself, excluding all boundaries and exploring all possibilities.

Examine, take a break, re-examine: use what's in the world to help you. If you chose exotic fish, where can you go to study, explore, discover, participate, even become one of these creatures? If an idea seems silly or impossible, take a good, long look at that one and invent ways of making it a reality. Let your imagination pour out; often ridiculous things prove to be the most inspiring and exciting.

Stoke your imagination's furnace with images: inspire yourself with imagery. Cut out pictures from magazines, take your camera on an outing, take pictures related and not related to your idea. If it's exotic fish, photograph not only sea life, but also billboards, cars, planes, pet-supply stores, or anything that fits the category.

Mix up the pictures, then assemble the images in a way that tells a story. If an image just doesn't fit, consider it a challenge. Virtually no one would put the image of a tropical fish on the same "idea table" as a billboard. But, what if a lonely tropical fish in a fishbowl looked out the pet store window and fell in love with an image on the billboard? Can you see a fun story developing?

Always add "Magic." In your imagination, there are no rules. The laws of gravity do not apply and fish can talk. There is magic in starting anywhere with things that interest you and making your idea anything and everything you want it to be.

Steps in the Write Direction

Michael

Michael Sprout

Senior Concept Writer, Concept Development

I'm a writer. And you know what the most difficult part of my job is? Writing.

Often it involves coming up with something to write about: a new concept, a new twist on an old concept, or an old concept that seems like a new twist on an old concept.

Let's say you're me. You're in a meeting about something. People are talking. You're trying to pay attention but the loose button on your sleeve needs your attention. Time goes by. Suddenly someone says to you, "Can you write something up by next Tuesday?"

"Sure." You say.

Why did you say "Sure"? Because it's Step I.

Step I. Say "Sure." When facing any new challenge, be fearless. Or at least appear so. As somebody once said, screenwriter William Goldman or philosopher Socrates maybe: nobody knows anything. But nobody ever admits that, so don't you start. Just take your assignment quietly to your office and sit down.

Step 2. Panic. This is a very important step in the creative process. There are a lot of negative feelings lurking around in that head of yours, and now is the time to let them out.

"I don't know what I'm doing." "What am I doing?" "I'm not fooling anyone." "I should have been a carpet installer."

Feel better? If you ever meet anyone without negative feelings, run the other way real fast.

Step 3. Go to the Library. This quaint reference to a building full of books simply means that you should gather as much information as possible about your subject matter. I once had to develop a theme park attraction about television. So I watched a lot of television, leafed through a lot of books with pictures of televisions and television shows in them, and talked to a lot of people who watch a lot of television.

The idea is to get your head so full of information that you can think of little else. Gorge yourself. Go off on tangents. Follow your interests. Nothing is off-limits. When your head is full, stop. Now comes the fun.

Step 4. Goof around. This can mean anything. Go to the movies. Hang around people you find funny. Make an interesting dinner your mother would disapprove of. Get distracted, because while you are distracting the conscious part of your brain, the really hardworking part goes into high gear.

You must not consciously think about your concept at this point. Seriously. It's like trying to bite into a raw oyster. If you try to grab ahold of your idea, it could get away from you, shoot out of your mouth, and land in someone else's lap.

Step 5. Go to sleep. This is really just a continuation of Step 4, but often necessary. Sometimes you can skip Step 5, but you never know.

Step 6. Let it happen. This part is a bit tricky. If you have ingested enough facts, figures, opinions, and various bits of useful and useless information, a mysterious process will almost certainly take place inside your head.

The VP in charge said, "And we need a show about television. That's right up your alley. See what you can do."

"Sure," I said, and went back to my office, put my head between my knees, and tried to figure out which alley he was talking about and how I ended up in it.

And then one evening at home, while I was in the, you know, smallest room in the house, an idea came to me and I had to write it down. Since the only paper handy was two-ply and perforated, I asked my wife to bring me a pad of paper. A few minutes later, I had a pretty good idea to present to the VP in our next meeting. Of course it was up to a large crew of very talented creative people to develop the idea and actually make it happen, but a big chunk of my work was done.

Step 7. Keep writing implements handy at all times. Paper, pencil, crayon, computer, coal, the back of a shovel, whatever. You'll need twenty-four-hour access. The need to record one's creative impulses often occurs while asleep. Never let these moments go by. Always get up and write them down. These moments are a gift to you from your own brain. Do not miss out. They melt away like an early frost in the morning unless you have a record to prove to your brain that you mean business.

And that's it. Have faith. With every project you do, you'll be taking these steps over and over again, but it will seem different, and a bit scary, every time.

Start with a Question

Dave Crawford

Principal Mechanical Engineer, Show/Ride Engineering

Start with a question to discover if there is an opportunity for creativity.

Questions start the creative process by asking how, why, and in what other way can something be done. The answers explore options that kick off creativity.

A job requiring an employee to do a specific task is designed for repetition. The answers to the how, why, and what other way questions would be information queries defining the task. Now, imagine a job that asks you to build a device that will allow someone to jump fifty feet into the air. This job is designed for options—asking how, why, and what other ways might there be will initiate the creative process.

> **Imagine how many different ways someone can jump fifty feet into the air. You're not constrained by cost, time, or even physics at this point. Let your mind wander from supersize trampolines to liquid fuel jetpacks. Let your curiosity lead you. Ask yourself the how, why, and what-other-ways questions. Get as many options down on paper as possible.**

The most unrealistic options inspire tangent ideas that take you to new places you would never have considered.

Process Questions

Kathy Mangum
Executive Producer/Vice President

No matter how big the challenge or how small, our process is the same. We apply critical thinking, ask basic questions to get started, and challenge our assumptions.

Before starting a project, I review the questions that need to be asked. It's an internal thought process that helps me decide what form the project will take and what kind of team it will require.

> Define or describe the creative challenge. Identify and make a list of the questions you need answered, starting with the most important: what problem am I solving? Who am I solving it for? What result do I want? Who are the right people to work with me? Next, add those questions that are specific to your challenge. Take the list to others and review it with them. Listen for questions you hadn't considered. Challenge your assumptions. When the questions are answered and your assumptions are in place, you're ready to solve the problem.

For example, Imagineers will be completely renovating an attraction at Walt Disney World in Florida that includes a new storyline. As we develop the idea further, we need to constantly question and challenge our own assumptions. Is the storyline appropriate to the attraction's location? Will the idea work with the available technology? What is the best way to tell the story—film, special effects, Audio-Animatronics, or all of the above?

It's like having a blank sheet of paper with lines on it or an exercise in connecting the dots. You know sizes and shapes and that the walls can't move! Knowing the parameters of the challenge and the questions that you have to answer allow you to work more effectively.

You Want to Be Creative

Chuck Ballew
Senior Concept Designer, Creative Development

To be creative, believe that you are and accept that your talents and skills will start at zero. Have fun. If creativity becomes a chore, you'll give up.

Use the best materials you can afford, but think of them as worthless.

Make a lot of mistakes. Do a ton of worthless testing. Use up paper and pencils, paint and brushes, water and glue—whatever you need.

Learn techniques. You will need to understand all aspects of your craft. Take classes, read books, talk to others who already do it, observe and analyze examples.

Fun comes first, rules come second. Stay engaged and excited about the creative process. Whenever I do an assignment, I inject something interesting and fun for me into it while following the stated goals.

Open your eyes. Creative people feast their eyes on the world. They are inspired by how things go together.

Don't be hard on yourself. Stop beating yourself up whenever you do something you hate. You're learning. The creative people you love developed their talent after a lot of learning, trial, and error.

Share your stuff. Show your work to people around you. You'll be surprised at the encouragement you'll receive. Most people want to be creative, but think they can't. Show them that all it takes is effort, fun, and confidence!

Do what you want. Do what interests you. The only rules are those you choose to follow. All the greatest talents made up their own rules, so why not you?

I express my creativity as an artist. If you want to be an artist, too, add the following to the list:

Learn perspective. This is a technique for creating depth and distance in a picture using vanishing points and horizon lines. It will help you draw realistically. Take classes or read books to learn.

Draw everything. Draw things all around you all the time. When you draw something, your brain remembers how to draw it in the future.

Process Practice

Sue Bryan
Senior Show Producer, Creative Development

*An exceptional concept depends on good process
as well as pure inspiration.*

Being aware of the design process and knowing what phase the team and the idea are in is a big part of the show producer's job. Inspiration generates ideas, and the process helps to shape efforts in a way to keep the team moving towards a fully developed idea.

Get going. Toss a bunch of ideas out. Direction often comes from joyous chaos.

Get excited. Brainstorm. Dream. Take tangents. Notice where ideas go, what's cool about them, and incorporate this into the design.

Get committed. Set up a regular project meeting time, discuss ideas, or just sit and stare at the wall. Ideas will come either way.

Get doughnuts or cookies. Brainstorming sessions go better when food or toys are around.

Get different opinions. Listen to someone else's point of view and listen for things that improve the design.

Get confused. Ask yourself hard questions that you can't answer.

Get stuck. Use your frustration to talk to more people, step back, and think about other options.

Get unstuck. Try a different direction. Throw out an impossible solution. Debating a wrong answer can help reveal the correct one.

Get your hands dirty. Build a rough model or stage a reading. You will learn more from this than from any debate, and you'll learn it in time to fix things.

Get reactions. Show the idea to others. Listen to what they say, especially if it isn't what you want to hear.

Get it on paper. Take everything you've learned and write a description of the goals and details of the design. If you write convincingly, you've probably got a great idea.

*If everyone is comfortable with the process, the team members
have the freedom to generate the best ideas for their project.*

Establishing Objectives

Barry

Barry Braverman
Senior Vice President, Creative Development

*Objectives are about choices that determine
a project's success or failure.*

A classic design problem, such as planning a child's birthday party, involves pragmatic considerations, artistic/creative opportunities, and financial and schedule constraints. Identifying objectives is a valuable exercise when planning a project.

> Make a list of your project's objectives. Write them down as they come to mind, rank them according to importance, and asterisk the objectives that would invalidate the purpose of the project if not met.
>
> Take the highest-priority objective, expand it with a list of subobjectives, then expand the next. As you complete the first two or three, a broad outline of a creative concept will emerge. From this, write a description of the final project, even if it is still vaguely defined.

For example, objectives for Bobby's Birthday Party might be:
1. Bobby and his friends feel his party was the best he has ever had.
2. I want help in planning and hosting the party so I can enjoy it.
3. Bobby's younger sister, Debbie, is to feel included but must not embarrass Bobby.

The first objective is pretty broad. Subobjectives would then be used to ensure its realization. The following subobjectives will enable Bobby to feel his party was the best ever.
   a. His friends "thumb's up" the party.
   b. The people he cares most about attend.
   c. He receives the new video game system he wants.

By articulating the subobjectives, a creative vision of the event begins to take form. How Bobby's friends judge the party will be a big factor in how he feels and will influence the theme. What's *in* with thirteen-year-olds—pirates or skateboards? If you skateboard, is there a skate park nearby? What are the safety concerns? Would all the guests participate? These objectives and subobjectives provide a basis for considering, accepting or rejecting various options.

*By articulating and prioritizing objectives, invaluable time and effort
is given to the planning phase of the project, ensuring its success.*

Working from the back end is finding the lessons that you don't want to learn in the midst of your project.

This practice of back end visualization is not limited to my profession; it is essential to almost everything we do and can be adapted to any project.

Next, consider how you could minimize these challenges so they do not negatively impact the project, and take necessary preventive action. This might be done through a contract (as I do it), through people you might hire, materials you might use, or by adjusting a schedule.

Imagine all the reasonably possible outcomes of the project, select the one that best meets your needs, think through all things that could delay, detour, or diminish your outcome and write them down.

For example, no matter how carefully we plan a construction project, changes will likely be necessary during the building process. This is addressed in the contract by including a mechanism to deal with these changes, thereby greatly reducing the possibility of disputes—a dose of preventive law.

Before coming to Imagineering, I was often in court trying to resolve contract disputes favorably for my clients. It was a valuable experience because I quickly learned that the most difficult and rancorous disputes typically occur where the parties have not thought about what would happen if things do not go exactly as they have planned. A good drafter of contracts practices preventive law.

I practice law at Imagineering. This, in fact, requires much creativity and forethought if one is to keep his or her sanity, so I always start at the end with my desired result and work backwards.

Anticipating the possible outcomes of everyday decisions before you make them helps to avoid calamities, not to mention inconveniences.

Peter Steinman
Vice President - General Counsel

Starting at the End

Building the Creative Toy Chest

Maggie Elliott

Retired Senior Vice President, Creative Development Administration

Currently: Full-Time Artist and Community Arts Developer

A creative toy chest stimulates thinking and exercises creative muscles.

To fill your toy chest, you get to go shopping. If you love to shop, here are some new places to explore. If you hate shopping, good! This will take you out of your comfort zone and inspire you in a challenging way. Get ready to shop till you drop.

Our first stop is your own personal *Mind Exploratorium*. Take some time to answer these questions, and then toss the answers in your toy chest.

What is my goal?

What is my purpose?

Can I define who I am?

What are my personal ethics?

Next on our shopping expedition is the *Learning Shop*. Here you get to pick up skills in interacting with others. Enjoy your adventure . . .

Am I visual and respond better to pictures?

Am I verbal and respond better to words?

For example: is it easier to follow a picture map or written directions?

Do I really listen and hear what is being said to me?

Am I formulating my response while hearing key words?

For example: the English language is filled with words that have double meanings. Are you hearing the meaning intended? Also, we have different definitions for the same word. Is your definition the same as the one transmitted?

Do I honestly respect different approaches to problem solving?

If I must, will I take the path others suggest?

Do I respect the individuality of my team members?

Am I a strong communicator?

Do I prefer to be with people to gain energy to create, or do I prefer to be alone while gathering energy?

More toys for my toy chest. What fun!

Now we are off to the *Auto Dealership*. What vehicle will I choose to tell the story? Story can be taken literally or as a metaphor. For example: do you write and/or talk in one of the following styles? Have fun choosing your auto.

Traditional: you emphasize reportage.

Impressionistic: you emphasize suggestions and hints.

Expressionistic: you emphasize feelings and emotions.

Abstract: you emphasize theory and the nonrepresentational.

What will the interior of your vehicle be?

Sentimental • Controversial • Intellectual • Subtle • Obvious • Playful

Experimental • Expressive • Aggressive • Passive • Dramatic

Is your toy chest getting full? Here's a secret: the toy chest can be as big as you need it to be. You can add as much as you like.

Now we are off to the *Research Center* to look for the following items. See if you can find them and their use for your project.

Find a telescope to reach beyond your limitations.

Invest in a magnifying glass to study detail.

Find your comfort zone and move out of it.

Don't bother picking up Avoidance. It's precisely the thing to avoid.

Think about "it." "It" is your contribution to the project.

Write about "it." Buy a compass and view "it" from all directions—upside-down and inside out. Critique "it."

Finally, your last store to visit is the *Beyond the Limits* shop. Here you can buy all kinds of wonderful things.

Permission to imagine the unimaginable.

Location of the keys you need to start your vehicle.

New skills for listening, building, and strengthening your communication abilities.

Respect for differences in ideas, people, and problem solving.

New areas to go shopping.

Pull out these toys to play the game of creativity. With each one, you will discover a different aspect of the creative process and multiple ways of expressing your own creativity. This is the object of playing the creative game.

Getting Into the Idea Zone

Many ideas lurk inside a plate of cookies!

Jam on ideas while driving. Turn off the car radio and tune in new ideas instead of jammin' to radio tunes when you are commuting. Let your brain fill the silent void with great ideas or solutions to challenges. Crank up the volume on your brainpower. Listen for ideas. It'll be music between your ears!

—Jason Grandt
Graphic Designer
Creative Development

Ideas come when they are ready and we are receptive.

We recognize ideas as they form in our imagination, but often for the unexpected or unusual ideas, the logical and judgmental aspects of our recognition system need to be preoccupied with other duties for these ideas to be considered. This is what happens when we are driving, exercising or dreaming.

Great ideas can happen when driving to work in the morning, because the pressure is off.

Before you start your commute, identify the day's tasks. Suggest to yourself that you're creatively relaxed and ready to find solutions. Then focus on the mechanical business of driving to work. Have no expectations and no notions of brilliance. Just let your creative mind go wandering for the perfect solutions.

—Gary Landrum
Associate Show Producer
Show Awareness
Walt Disney Imagineering Florida

The Creative You

Arden Ashley
Sr. Principal Set Decorator, Environmental Design & Engineering

*Creativity is about options and decisions that
we make on a daily basis.*

We start our day making creative decisions: the tastes we assemble for breakfast or the colors and style of clothing we choose to wear for the day's events.

Every day is filled with myriad decisions as to decorating personal or work space, listening to music, or reading books. Even the cars we drive are a reflection of our creative selves revealing how we think, feel, and solve problems. To become more aware of your creative self make a personal storyboard, a visual display of all the things that express who you are, to tell your creative story.

*Supplies: Scissors, glue, tape, note cards, pushpins, large corkboard
or 8½" x 11" or larger notebook, and writing utensil.*

Start by using a large corkboard or, if space is limited, a notebook. Cut out, group, and display the ideas and images that you are drawn to or passionate about from magazines, books, photographs; use samples of colors, textures, or fabrics, as well as making your own sketches and notes. Be sure to include music, poems, quotes, and other written information. The wider the variety of materials and images, the more it will define your creative self and stimulate your creativity.

Once your images are gathered and attached, put your personal storyboard in a place where you will see it daily and draw inspiration from it.

*Your personal storyboard will never be complete.
As you learn, grow, and change, feel free to edit those things
that are no longer of interest to you and add your
new experiences and ideas.*

Creativity requires taking everything you know and using it differently.
—Susan Dain

Casting for Ideas

Todd Camill

Mechanical Engineer, Show/Ride Engineering

Looking for those good ideas? Somewhere among your current, old, wild, and unreasonable ideas are good ideas waiting to be discovered.

To catch that elusive big fish, you probably wouldn't drop a hook at your feet, hoping it had already found you. You would cast far away into the deeper, murkier waters and then reel back in. Trolling for new ideas is the same. You won't find them hanging around your current ideas. You need to cast your thinking far out, farther than you think is reasonable or feasible.

Ponder your creative challenge and brainstorm its most amazing unlimited incarnation. Expand on the concept with details.

Reel in your idea with some real-world thinking. How can you accomplish some or most of your ultimate idea, given its limitations? What's easy? What's hard? What works? What are you left with when you're back to reality?

Continue brainstorming, expanding, and reeling in a little reality with your challenge by casting your ultimate vision in different directions.

Sort your catch. Identify any novel ideas in the middle ground of reasonableness and focus on those. These ideas breathe on their own.

The point is to find the great doable ideas along the way, while breaking the creative mind out of what it already knows and moving it to new possibilities.

Permission to be awkward and weird granted!

—Mk Haley

"One of the advantages of being disorderly is that one is constantly making exciting discoveries."

—A.A. Milne

The more you know, the more you are able to do.

—Luc Mayrand

The Sketchbook

Ethan Reed

Show Animator and Designer, Show Animation & Programming

To help your brain soak everything and everyone up,
keep a sketchbook handy.

Since attending college to study animation, I have never been without a sketchbook. It goes everywhere with me. I draw the people around me, studying their gestures and ways of walking as well as how they react to the environment. I learn from observation and record what I learn.

You might think that keeping a sketchbook is just for artists who can draw. However, its purpose is to develop your powers of observation so it doesn't matter if you draw stick figures or highly detailed portraits. Sketching is an essential creative discipline for engineers, musicians, writers, lawyers, and artists—and you.

> Buy a sketchbook that's the perfect size for you to take with you everywhere. Sketch those wonderful fascinating moments that you see or hear. Draw them no matter your level of skill. If you feel you really can't draw, then invest in a camera, to take pictures of anything that interests you and keep notes on it. Keep in mind that a camera can be considered intrusive by some and discretion is appropriate when photographing individuals or groups (landscapes, however, love to be photographed).

When you have a sketchbook, you'll never need to look for a
napkin to sketch on again.

The Idea Journal

Bill West

Senior Software Engineer, Scientific Systems, Show/Ride Engineering

If you're more comfortable with writing than sketching,
keep a journal.

The idea journal is the written version of the sketchbook. It captures words and word images that you see and feel in both sweeping generalities and specific details. It's a personal log for your ideas and a way to make sure a fabulous idea doesn't disappear.

> Purchase the ideal journal for your lifestyle, be it a Palm Pilot or similar PDA, notepad, sticky notes, or voice recorder. Take it with you wherever you go. Although if you get enough flashes of inspiration in the shower, you'll need to consider options that are waterproof!
>
> Use the journal as a resource, regularly reviewing the ideas, notions, scenarios, and information you are capturing. Ask yourself: how am I using my journal? What do I want to keep as a memory frozen in word images? What can I expand into a story, or work or home project?

Keep in mind that ideas are generally fleeting and must be captured
as they arise. Some will hang around and let you mull them over,
but most are like a flash of lightning and need instant attention.

Like age has become irrevelant, the seasons no longer seem a marker of potential weather.

The weather's now like the N season — anything could happen at any time of year.

Pausing is not an option in New York.

Snow:
Kernels in an air popper
balls in a lottery machine

...with a scowl on his face

Rain dancing on the roof like the Radio City Rockettes.

Cat-paw-sized drops padding down the windshield

Rain pouring down like a Brita water filter with a chip in the lid.

Rain so thick - it's opaque.

A rainbow of umbrellas when the rain starts.

Rain being blown across the sky like puffs of white smoke.

In his shiny polished shoes
And his shiny pressed pants
Sitting prim, sitting proper
In the prim proper dance

obtuse & oblique
NO,
obtuse & opaque

His brow creased deeper
and his lips compressed
into a thin line!
Compressed in disapproval.

waspishly   owlishly

43

Skills to Match Creativity

Steve Kawamura
Manager, Communications

A wild, wonderful idea demands more of you than just having it.
Creativity and skill need each other.

There is a significant difference between creativity and skill that often goes unnoticed. Imagineers are responsible for coming up with imaginative and engaging ideas, but they are also required to maintain a high level of discipline and technical skill in addition to their creative talents.

> **Identify the creative abilities and skills you use for expressing your creativity. Make a three-column list. One is for your creative abilities, such as a gift for coming up with big ideas, or for developmental and multidimensional thinking.**
>
> **Another is for the skills or talents that you use to express your ideas such as writing, drawing, or pitching ideas.**
>
> **The third column is for the abilities and skills that you will need to achieve future goals. Devise a plan for attaining these abilities and skills. Then do it! You'll be creating your future.**

Matching skills to creativity is essential for expressing ideas. For instance, Imagineers must communicate their ideas clearly and concisely to successfully pass the baton during the process of turning ideas into reality. To convey their ideas, artists draw or paint, architects and engineers use design software, developers draft site plans, financial analysts use spreadsheets, and filmmakers use editing programs to transform ethereal concepts into physical forms that can be copied, transported, shared, discussed, and debated. All these tasks require highly developed skills through which creativity is expressed.

By mastering the technical skill that best fits your field—be it drawing, computer programming, or modeling—you eliminate barriers, allowing ideas to emerge and your brain to storm furiously.

Idea Diary

Marshall Monroe
Former Creative Director. Currently: Visioning Consultant

For a way to engage your conceptual ability and showcase the connection between storytelling and the creative process, keep an Idea Diary.

Start with a sheet of paper, a pen, and note cards. Draw a circle in the middle of the paper and write your project's name. At the top, write *Current Situation: Observations.* In a radial pattern around the circle, write your project's current attributes and challenges. Be observant and honest; look outward, look inward, and look for variety.

At the top of a bigger paper or on a big pin board or, best of all, on a whole wall, tack up a note card entitled *Preferred Situation: Attributes.* On more note cards, identify your big-concept attributes, including awards, honors, or achievements. Pin them up.

Get some magazines or catalogues, a pair of scissors, and a big glue stick. Cut out images and descriptions that capture the feeling of what you want to achieve. Mix, match, and attach them to the paper, grouping similar images. Add descriptive words. You're creating your project's world.

For example, make a journal entry that begins "Dear Idea Diary" or "Captain's Log: Star Date . . ." or whatever you like. Write from the perspective of a wide-eyed, open-minded person from another country who has just stumbled across the new world you have created a thousand years from now. Write your story, painting a word picture by capturing all aspects of your created world in colors, sights, and sounds.

Read it to others: spouse, friend, colleagues, or team members. Enter more ideas, reflect on them, and add images that capture your end result. Your images and diary story will give you the information you need to materialize your ideas.

Ideas are future-form information that becomes reality.
Story is the ultimate way to record and recall this information.

Listen to Quiet "Head Chatter"

Bernie

Bernie Mosher

Director, Creative Development Services, Walt Disney Imagineering Florida

To quiet your own "head chatter" so that your ideas and others can be heard, focus on listening.

"Head chatter," the ongoing commentary of our inner voice, can become so loud and intense that we are consumed by it. If it is negative, we are most often worrying about something out of our control, or we are lost in circular thinking that has no apparent end. With "head chatter," our listening is focused on our internal voices. External listening can break the intensity of "head chatter," letting us hear our thoughts, ideas, and what others have to say.

> Sit quietly. Listen to all the existing environmental sounds, including the ones we don't usually hear, such as the buzz of an overhead light, the air conditioner, or your own breath. Focus on listening rather than thinking; let conversations fade into the background and listen to all the surrounding sounds. Focus on your internal listening mechanism and what you are hearing externally.

Not only is this exercise good for quieting your own "head chatter" when you need to listen to others, it also helps me to switch gears after I have been multitasking, or when I am going to do brainstorming meetings or other intense activities.

The more you focus on listening, the less "head chatter" you will hear.

Listening for Ideas

Bradlee

Bradlee Snow
End User Computer Support Information Services Senior

*Support the creative needs of others and
learn about their challenges by listening.*

Listening is an art in itself; it certainly is a discipline with principles, where focusing on what the speaker is saying and resisting the temptation to form responses while others are speaking is paramount. You can ask a lot of questions but should not interrupt the answers. Save the formation of your own idea until you have heard what the speaker has to say.

In order to generate ideas, the imagination must have enough information available to form solutions. Listening is one of our sensory resources for gathering information for problem solving. The more information we gather, the more ideas we have.

Listen with the intent of helping someone get his or her job done more efficiently and economically. To help them accomplish their goal, identify what is currently available and consider what is on the horizon that might be used. Decide who can build on the ideas, can see what is possible, and will know how to make it happen. Then you can take action.

I listen for ideas because I want to help Imagineers do what they do so well and listening stimulates my technical creativity. It helps me to contribute to putting the smiles on guests' faces, and that was my reason for becoming an Imagineer in the first place.

Listening for ideas assures that you'll have them.

I didn't know it would do that!
—John Polk, Manager, Image & Effects

A good, vigorous run or even a leisurely walk can clear the head, open the mind, and open receptivity to thought. It's like daydreaming on your feet.

· Exercise alone. It's the only way to focus your mind.
· Leave the music at home. It's hard to concentrate with too many distractions (especially those of your own making).
· Get into a rhythm and let your mind wander.
· It's okay if you don't think about the things you want to, you may be pleasantly surprised by something that comes completely out of the blue.
· It's hard to write your ideas down while exercising. Once you've hit on an idea or a solution, let it stay with you until you are through. Then all you have to worry about is sweating all over the paper while writing it down.

—Dave Fisher
Senior Show Writer
Creative Development

When you're a passenger in a car or on a train, you can slip into a daydreaming mode and focus on your assignment.

Think everything through. Be mechanical: collect all the data associated with the creative problem, thoroughly assess it, present the data internally, and mentally ask for the solution. (One problem at a time, please.)

Then for the hardest part: Don't think about it any more. Just wait for the solution.

—Doris Hardoon Woodward
Former Senior Show Producer

While insomnia is annoying, it can be seen as an opportunity to generate ideas or work through a daytime assignment. While lying in the calm of a dark room at night, ideas can freely tumble around in your imagination.

Most people fail to turn on the lights and in the morning find that two or three sentences are written on top of each other. Those brilliant world-saving or best-selling thoughts end up reading something like "Exoer becise tan merquep op u thirguinet." Cryptographers should decipher this as "Buy a penlight!"

—Jody Revenson
Editor, Disney Editions

Dreams can help express ideas with confidence in your waking life. When sleeping, the brain is very busy dreaming, thinking, and problem solving.

Before going to sleep, set the intention of being braver and more adventurous with your ideas. Think of something that you couldn't possibly do, such as flying, when you're aware you've started to dream, tell yourself, *I can do anything right now.* Give yourself permission to be free of fear, gravity, or ridicule. Slowly look around in your dream, knowing that anything you want can happen. Take action on your wish, accomplish it, and translate your success into your waking life.

Once I was running in a dream, but I really wanted to fly. I thought to myself, "You know you can do it, you can fly." And I did! I flew over a field at any speed I wanted and even went through a hole in a fence. It was so natural that I realized I could always do it. When I woke up from this dream, I felt a new level of self confidence. It stayed with me during the day, and at work I was more confident than ever in expressing my ideas.

If this exercise doesn't work for you, encourage yourself to be more courageous and adventurous in expressing your ideas right before you go to sleep and as often as you can in your waking life.

— Susan Zavala,
Visual Communications Rep., Creative Development

Combining Ideas

Bill

Bill Willcox

Principal Engineer, Ride Mechanical Systems

For a quick method for generating ideas, start with the tried and true.

Combining ideas develops new ones and strengthens concepts, stories, or creative solutions. It can be very effective in brainstorming when unrelated ideas are put together. The following method is a fast way to combine seemingly different ideas into new ones.

> On one sheet of paper, list in a single column all your ideas of interest, for example all the rides in every Disney theme park. Make a copy of the list. Place each list side by side and then slide them up and down with respect to one another until interesting, plausible, or useful combinations start popping up. Such a combination might be Indiana Jones™ meets Peter Pan. Once you select a combination, start exploring the relationship between the two elements. What might they have in common? Why are they so popular? Why would they never get along?

The method can be automated, of course, but it is much more fun when you slide the sheets of paper by hand.

The Idea Mixer

What's Brainstorming All About?

Mk Haley
Technology Resources Manager, Image and Effects

What is brainstorming?

Brainstorming is a process that incites creative solutions with riotous, swirling activity, thunderclaps of genius, and sweeping winds of change.

We brainstorm to resolve challenges with a purposefully unstructured structure providing one or more viable solutions. The structure behind brainstorming allows creative chaos to flourish.

Tools:

Brainstormers: a group of three to twelve people, of any age or expertise; diversity is essential.

Moderator: to keep things flowing

Runner: to help record concepts, pin up cards, and organize ideas

Supplies: index cards, magic markers, pushpins

Place: comfortable, easy access to supplies, pinable wall surface

Rules:

There are no bad ideas: one idea leads to another.

Respect all input: expect different contributions.

Share the imperfect things: someone might be inspired.

Record every idea: even if stated more than once, it might mean something.

Be willing to be wrong.

Set meeting time limits: you'll know when to stop.

Ready, Set, Brainstorm!

Define the challenge. Are you designing a lemonade stand, looking for a summer job, or trying to get rid of lemons? Avoid stating solutions.

State your challenge. This is the moderator's task.

Get busy. Propose that first word or question, for example: lemonade! Encourage responses. Using cards, capture and connect ideas, emotions, things, places, times, memories, technology, history, business, etc.

Collect ideas for another twenty minutes. Sort into piles and categories. Are there consistent themes? Any holes that need filling? If so, the moderator should address these needs.

Keep going. Brainstorming is a circular process. You do, you learn, you do again from what you've learned, and repeat.

Time's up! The wall looks a mess: cards with terrible handwriting, bad doodles, all connected to each other in an organic-looking hierarchy.

Brainstorming is done. How can that be?—there's no solution. Yes, there is—in the connections or the innovations.

Now, for the ninety-nine percent perspiration that brings innovation to fruition, follow up with research, implementation, building, testing, and installation.

It Just Takes a Spark

Rhonda Counts

Show Producer, Walt Disney Imagineering Florida

To spark the creativity of others, you need to find that spark first.

In facilitating brainstorming sessions, I find myself focusing on a word, phrase, or image that gets the thought process going and the energy flowing. It isn't really an idea; it's the spark of one. This is the creative moment I have in helping to lead the team to the goal.

Immerse yourself in the subject matter as many ways as possible before the brainstorming session and then start asking questions. For example, if your brainstorming topic is to develop a themed family event, immerse yourself in the theme by reading books and watching movies or television shows related to the theme. Pay attention to the stories, words, or images that have meaning for you. Immerse yourself in the environment: visit the intended location or a similar one and imagine what could take place, paying close attention to details that capture your interest. What sparks you has the potential to spark others.

Ask yourself, what excited me? Was it a color, emotional tone, or object? Will it excite the team? What entertained me? Was it the theme, story action, or a visual effect? Will it entertain the team? In answering these questions, look for a spark to ignite the ideas of others. If you are energized and enthusiastic, you will find it.

Think about how you felt when a spark was passed on to you. When it happens—wham!—ideas start to flow. It is as important to spark ideas as it is to have them.

What Sparks Me?

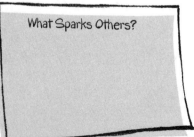

What Sparks Others?

Blurt It Out

Dave

David McCartney

Principal Mechanical Engineer, Show/Ride Engineering

In brainstorming sessions, it helps to be prepared in order to have ideas ready to offer.

Recently, I was in a brainstorming session dedicated to design additions for a ride vehicle. The vehicle was small, with no room to hide complex mechanisms inside the body. Moreover, the additions had to blend with the vehicle's theming. We were standing there, staring at the vehicle without a clue where to start, when the project leader encouraged us to just blurt our ideas out. It triggered a flow of ideas and before long we had a list of twenty-five possible solutions.

Whenever possible, I like to prepare for these sessions and use a system for collecting ideas.

Supplies: file, paper, a pen or pencil, and a willingness to capture your ideas

Create a file and put your ideas in it as they come to you. Organization is not paramount. Just get the ideas written down before they get away. Keep the file open so that you can add to it easily. Visit the file often, especially before participating in a brainstorming session.

This file helps me with my projects and work; in fact, I kept ideas for *this* book in it. You just never know when someone will ask you for an idea!

Let the Absurd Lead the Way

Chris Runco

Senior Concept Designer, Creative Development

Inspired by Craig Wilson, former Imagineer

In brainstorming, the weirdest, wackiest ideas are often the ones that break down walls to originality. That's why the "there are no bad ideas" rule is so important.

Even if ideas are too ridiculous or dumb to survive, just hanging with them for consideration can loosen us up. Then, we can stretch farther to find the ideas that will really work.

> Make a list of objects relating to your project. Look at each object and think of something else. Think of something that has absolutely nothing to do with the object and write its name next to the object. For example, on my water-ride project, looking at the boat, I thought about the polka; for the grizzly bear, lipstick came to mind; and for the elegant oak tree, I thought Swedish meatballs! Got it?

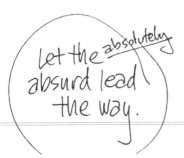

Let the _absolutely_ absurd lead the way.

Holding the unrelated images in mind, develop a series of questions that connect the two. For example: what does the boat engine sound like? What color is the bear's fur? What is the sound of wind rustling through the meatballs? Does it splatter the gravy?

Build a project-idea scenario using this information. For example, for me to design a water effect, I would ask, "Would it be in the cool shade of an oak tree, with water dripping off the leaves making a sound as it plops into a pond like gobs of gravy to the rhythm of a polka beat?" Is the absurd leading the way yet?

Nothing should seem too ridiculous to consider.

You can't tell an artist when to have an idea or how many to have.
—John Hench

How We Really Come Up with Ideas . . .

George Scribner
Creative Director, Theme Park Productions

The next day . . .

Techniques

Nobody wants to be mediocre. Only the mediocre person is always at his best. You have to fail. You have to take risks.

—Jan O'Connor
Show Writer, Creative Development

Find the time of day when you work best. Ignore the clock... some work best at night, some early in the morning.

—Scot Drake
Principal Concept Designer
Creative Development

Start on a task and just don't give up... keep at it!

—Mark Huber
Technical Staff
WDI Research & Development

OK, how tough can it be? Use fear as a motivator, not as an inhibitor.

—Neil Engel
Show Designer
Creative Development

Creativity is Learning!

Ginnie

Ginnie Gallo
Assistant Librarian, Information Research Center, Creative Development

Inspired by Lucia Capacchione

If you feel awkward, uncomfortable and a bit foolish, you might be on the edge of a creative breakthrough or learning something new.

The joy of creating (also its curse) is being a lifelong learner. Creating puts you face to face with the new or the unknown which can leave you feeling awkward and on the verge of frustration. It challenges the comfort and the sophistication of what we know. Computer software upgrades, the new accounting system, changes in management, or taking on a new assignment can return us to instant learner status, where creative opportunities abound. At Imagineering, we need to sustain learner status so that we can be creatively open, flexible, and responsive while leaping into the unknown.

> To find your learner status, write your full name on a piece of paper with your normal writing hand, and then write your full name with your other hand (your nondominant hand). Pay attention to how easily you can write the first signature and what effort it took to produce the second one. When writing with your other hand, ask yourself: what does it feel like (frustrating, silly, fun)? How long does it take? Does it require concentration? How is this like learning or creating?

Use this exercise when you need a quick reminder of how it feels to learn or to take a different point of view.

Sign your name with your normal hand.

Now sign your name with your other hand.

"I Know What I Like When I See It"

Sue Bryan

Senior Show Producer, Concept Development

Your ability to articulate your likes and dislikes will give you the ability to champion and defend your project.

To understand why you like something, you have to be a "design detective." If you are a committed detective, you will make notes and collect images, examples, and quotes on your own tastes for future reference.

Observe something you like for five to ten minutes. Notice your reactions: what aspects attract you—color, shape, sound, form, personality, or habit? What engages you—feeling, memories, details, or use? What makes you buy one product over another—desire, expense, practical need, or label?

Observe something you don't like for five to ten minutes. Notice your negative reactions but, more importantly, figure out why you don't like it. Are aspects such as cultural associations, materials, context, memories, or trendiness turning you off? Find something you do appreciate in these things. Almost everything is cool in someone's eyes—figure out why.

Knowing what you like and articulating why you like it are tools that can help you create a coherent, complex design.

Story Landscape

Michelle

Michelle Sullivan
Senior Landscape Architect, Landscape Architecture

Start with story to create exterior story environments.

I am a storytelling landscape architect for the Disney resorts and theme parks. My approach for developing story landscapes is similar to an actor preparing for a role. It works well with story-driven projects.

> **Find out everything about the story being created. Steep yourself in the role by researching the project's needs.**

For example, story landscapes need large specimen trees that we buy from nurseries or raise on one of our properties. I like to spend numerous hours in the library looking for written and visual clues or visiting inspiring locations similar to the one I am working on.

> **Develop the story, and your plan will take shape for gathering needed materials and casting players.**

For me, this means that my search for the plant material to support the story begins. The object is to find the right "player" (tree or other plant) for the right location. When I discover the right player, I feel extreme joy and maybe even do a little victory dance.

> **Assemble all the parts of your story project.**

In the assembly phase, landscaping starts with large cranes bringing in the bigger specimen trees. Seeing a large tree fly through the air in its box is both surreal and magical. As it comes down to earth with a final twist and review, the sides of the crate are removed, and the tree settles into a new home in the storytelling landscape. As the larger trees set down their roots and the smaller trees and foliage fall into place, I feel great satisfaction in preparing the set for the Guests who will themselves soon become part of the scene.

Consider story as a means for seeing your external living world in a new way. I see each living plant as more than a green object: it is a unique character with its own name and story.

Story Makers

Tom McCann

Senior Vice President, Engineering

What does it take to be a story maker?

Walt Disney explained it this way: "I dream, I test my dreams against my beliefs, I dare to take risks, and I execute my vision to make those dreams come true."

Imagineers prove this true by translating creative visions, stories, and artwork into real-life shows, rides, and facilities. In this way, one can think of engineers as story makers. Engineering's task is to make a creative concept come alive as a reality with technology and engineering.

The story we are telling and the need for performance reliability govern our efforts. Integration is a critical step in the process and takes us from the imagination with creative intent to the actual product, shape, and form. This process generates questions that apply to any project.

Ask: What is the story's intent? Should it feel like an earthquake? Should it feel like I'm in space?

During prototype development, ask: What have we learned through observation and trial and error? What physical limitations characterized the first attempts at the new concept?

Repeat the process, making adjustments and ask: Can we reduce the time factor?

In developing the concept, ask: What illustrations, models, and animation are necessary?

Then ask: Can the concept be brought to a reality as seen in the mind's eye and visually represented on paper? This is a true test not only of the story but of the story makers.

It takes consistency, courage, determination, and know-how, plus technology to work through these phases of reality testing.

Walt even acted out story scenarios for his staff.
—Dave Fisher

Seemingly common elements can elevate the story experience for beyond the conventional.
—Jason Surrell

65

Mad Tea Party—A Story Event

Jason

Jason Surrell
Show Writer, Walt Disney Imagineering Florida

If you're stuck planning the same old office event or it's your turn to host another annual holiday family get-together, do it differently—use story as the organizing principle.

Imagineers use story as the organizing principle for designing events for theme parks. Story allows you to make decisions based on established criteria. The flow of action tells you how to order the event elements, and the time and place will tell you how they can be visually represented. In the process, you become the storyteller and everyone at the event becomes a character in the story.

Decide what story you want to tell (the Guest experience). What will Guests do (the action)? Where will they do it (the setting)? When will it happen (date, time, even "period")? What do you want them to tell their friends the day after the event (the result)?

Write the flow of activities as if it were a script. Imagine every aspect of the event.

Make a list of the details that are absolutely necessary to tell the story, perhaps even cutting out images from magazines that represent your ideas. You now have the basic information needed to create a story-organized event.

For example, when planning an office retreat, tell the story of past or future successes in activities and themes such as an old-fashioned Western barbecue or a picnic with croquet and badminton. Plan a family event telling your family's story.

My mother uses story as an organizing principle to plan her annual holiday tea party. The story is about our family and the setting reflects her themes: a Christmas in Tuscany, a Cajun Christmas, even a Disney Christmas. She selects activities with distinct themes and adheres to those themes in every detail, from individual handcrafted place settings to carefully selected background music.

While planning, always refer to the story and ask: what will strengthen the story experience? Based on your answer, make decisions to cut, add, or revise as needed.

Recalibrating Normal

Will

Will Hastings
Designer, Environmental Design & Engineering

To create an alternate world, start with the real one.

As a lighting designer, I use a technique for selecting color palettes I call "Calibrating Normal." When picking colors for a room or for an outfit, it is important in lighting to create a palette of filter colors that go well with each other. When lighting a play, a film, or a themed environment, you're lighting another world whether it is a planet full of strange creatures and alien landscapes or the seedy underworld of gangsters. When lighting such worlds, I start with one simple question: what is normal?

Determine the baseline for normal. For example, in my Hong Kong hotel, the windows are tinted and the sky's light is a dusty gray with a touch of blue. Under an overcast sky, objects cast diffuse, almost non-existent shadows. At my home in Los Angeles, warm amber sunlight floods through the windows, filling the rooms and casting long, deep, nearly purple shadows.

In recreating either environment for a movie set, the baseline for normal would be different. What color would you use to simulate sunlight?

Create a world where the planet has a green sun and green sunlight is normal. Base your choices on the idea that green is the new white. Recalibrate normal from your new baseline. As a designer and storyteller, what questions arise: if the sun is green, what colors are the sky, shadows, ocean, plants, or people? These answers shape your new world.

You don't have to make up all the answers. Simply imagine (or research) how the laws of physics and logic would translate your normal into the new world, giving it continuity and believability.

We pay attention to our surroundings and the people in the spaces.
–John Mazzella

Some believe to be creative is to create the unbelievable.
–Chuck Flueck

Visual Storytelling Tool: Feeling

Leticia G. Lelevier
Senior Show Producer, Creative Development

Start with feeling and vision to create a visual story.

All the things that you feel and see contribute to your imagination's sensory vocabulary. You draw upon this vocabulary whenever you create; it is especially important when you are creating a visual story.

Getting a "feeling on the feeling" is a key element to visual storytelling. This means identifying early in the creative process the project's overall essence and emotion—the effect the project's story should radiate.

> List all the influences and stimuli around your project plus its characteristics. If your project is decorating a room, you might consider: who uses the room? What happens in it? What is its dominant feeling? What do people say about the room? What would the room say if it could talk? Review the list.
>
> Be perceptive. Put your senses to work capturing the spirit of your project's story or end result. What's the dominant feeling conveyed in your list? Name it. Write it down. Next, convert this feeling into sample images, sketches, photographs, colors, or graphic elements. You are creating a visual vocabulary from these samples that encompass your project's basic storytelling elements. You now have the feeling and image foundation for visualizing your project.

I've discovered that it's the image vocabulary derived from a dominant feeling that maintains visual unity throughout any project. Test it out by going to your favorite restaurant and to one you don't like. What's the difference in the dominant feelings conveyed? What would you describe as their visual vocabularies or the story experience they offer?

Visual Storytelling Tool: Vision

Cicero Greathouse

Art Director, Walt Disney Imagineering Florida

In visual storytelling the first step is to fully understand the story and the context of the situation.

Within the story is the vision, and the test of this vision is externalizing it. As the story develops, the vision provides the structure and visual unity that give the story its identity.

> Create a vision with a mental image that represents the project's story. Test the vision by externalizing it. Collect sketches, scripts, photographs, existing images, or information about the location that externalizes your vision. Study these external images and identify all the details. Now you are ready to think freely about creating solutions for developing, maintaining, or enhancing your project. Select the best ideas and mock up a detailed presentation. Make the presentation to those necessary, or, if you are in charge, review for selection (reviewing ideas in presentation format will let you evaluate them at their best).

I've learned that it's best to have a vision. Its underlying structure enables designers, production talent, or field art directors to stay within the intent of the story when making adjustments to the project or maintaining a completed one.

Pick Three Things

Mark Sumner

Senior Technical Director, Show/Ride Engineering

There's more to making up stories than just tucking the children in with a nighttime tale.

Forcing yourself to create a story with three unrelated things can help break down preconceived notions about how things ought to work and make you more comfortable exploring alternate possibilities that may lead to the next great idea. I learned this when my children were little and we played a story game, Pick Three Things. Their job was to pick seemingly unrelated things, and my job was to use them in a story. I would have to discover how the things they picked were connected or create a connection as I made up the story.

> **As the storyteller, gather your listeners whether children or adults. Have them think of three unrelated things that you will use in a story. No dictionaries allowed.**

Here is an example of a story I made up when my children chose a paper clip, the Man in the Moon, and George Washington:

Once upon a time, George Washington was sitting under a tree relaxing late in the evening. A little girl came up to him and asked, "Is the moon really made of green cheese?" George replied, "I don't think so!"

Just then a loud voice proclaimed, "I'm the Man in the Moon, and I'm made of green cheese, but I have crackers on my backside that you can't see!"

They'd never heard the moon talk; scared, they ran to see Benjamin Franklin. Ben was repairing his kite, which had been struck by lightning. They told him, "The Man in the Moon spoke!" Ben chuckled and explained, "Thomas Jefferson's in the woods practicing his lines for a play; he's playing the Man in the Moon."

After a good laugh, the little girl said, "This is a great story!" She sat down at Benjamin Franklin's desk and wrote it out. The story was three pages long. She announced, "I hope I don't lose any of the papers before I get home to show my mother!" Ben, being an inventor, thought for a moment and grabbed some wire. He bent the wire into a couple of loops, spread the loops slightly apart, then put the paper between the loops to hold the papers together.

Impressed, George Washington asked, "What do you call that, Ben?" Ben paused and said, "I'll call it a paper clip!"

Trust your imagination to find the connections between the items, to bring them to the surface, and to keep the story flowing. Your imagination is well trained in connecting information in many different ways. It's important to become more receptive to the unexpected connections—therein lies creativity.

To do this by yourself, write a story using three unrelated objects in your environment. Write continuously without stopping to think.

Let's see if
the idea flies!

Think in Adjectives

Steve Beyer
Senior Concept Designer, Creative Development

To breathe life into your projects and give your ideas emotional zing, think in adjectives.

Imagineers build emotional journeys for our guests in story environments. We begin by describing the story experience in adjectives that capture feelings and imaginations—especially our own. We think about the emotion we want to induce—scary, sunny, happy, exhilarating, tense, romantic—rather than focusing on building a roller coaster, theater, school, patio, or family room. If we feel the excitement, romance, or thrill that we are creating, our guests will feel it too. Adjectives are used in concept pitches as well as in storyboards, models, and mock-ups, and are infused into the final product. We are collectors of adjectives because they invite idea flow.

> **Make a list of the adjectives that you use to describe such feelings as love, fear, joy, and sadness. Then hunt for more. Find them in books, TV commercials, or magazine advertisements. Interview friends and family. Use the newfound adjectives in a sentence that describes your idea or project. Look for a good descriptive fit.**

For example: if you are transforming a bedroom into a family room, focus on the emotion you want to induce, such as joy. Make up a sentence using adjectives from your joy list; exchange adjectives in your sentence until you find the ones that capture the feeling you want in the room, then engage your imagination and let ideas flow. Test your choices on family and friends: what's their feedback? What did they experience? What changes do you need to make?

Adjectives set a mood, convey a message, and enhance reality. They are rooted in our emotional responses and evoke commonly shared images, tapping into our memory banks.

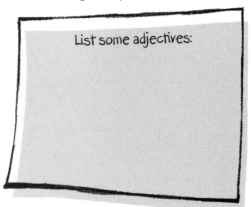

List some adjectives:

Think in Analogies

Tom Gilleon
Former Imagineer. Currently: Illustrator and Gallery Artist

You know what you want because you've seen or felt something like it before.

The analogy is a powerful, descriptive, creative tool for painting pictures that express ideas. If you want your backyard to look like an English garden by day and feel like Main Street, U.S.A., at Disneyland at night, you're conjuring images of herbs and flowers, little pathways, and surrounding trees by day, and tiny, sparkling lights floating in the trees surrounding the garden by night. Thinking analogically will help you realize your vision.

> Use the phrase, "It's like . . ." and observe your surroundings, relating your sensory experience to the things you want to create. For example, "My office is like an ice cream parlor on a warm day" suggests images of a friendly, colorful, cool place that has an enticing aroma. "My office is like a country doctor's office" conjures an image that is cozy, a little sparse, with wooden furniture, lace curtains, and potted plants.

Analogies will help you move from what something's like to an idea you are seeking to generate or communicate to others. For example, in describing the concept for the Indiana Jones Adventure™ vehicle, one could say that it is like an animated character. It moves along the track and responds emotionally to its surroundings, adding another layer of story experience for guests. In describing a process such as creativity, one could say that being creative is like breathing. Don't get caught up in formulas. Breathing is essential; you want to do it for a very long time. The longer you breathe, the more longevity you have, the more ideas you have.

List some analogies:

Analogies build the imagination's visual and emotional vocabulary. Collect them like pearls on a string. They have a familiarity about them that is reassuring.

Don't be afraid of possibilities!

"What If?"

Steve "Mouse" Silverstein
Principal Developer, Animation Programming Systems, Walt Disney Imagineering Florida

Use "What if?" to preface an idea or suggestion.

"What if?" was a favorite phrase of my Imagineering mentor, Wathel Rogers. Legend has it that he uttered the phrase so often while problem solving that it became his nickname! "What if?" has the nifty effect of inviting others to share their comments and opinions. It's like saying, "I'd really like to hear what you think about this."

> **Use the phrase for suggesting ideas to yourself and others.**
> **Use it to mean, "What makes the most magic happen?"**
> **Use it as a preface for exploring positive, creative ideas, and solutions,**
> **and it makes the most magic happen.**
> **Ask and respond to your own "What ifs?" List them. Stay positive.**
> **Think of a complete answer for each "What if?" question that you list.**

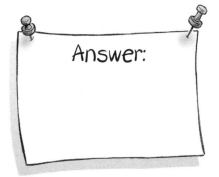

The benefits to putting the "What if?" phrase to work are:
- Keeps you open to any possible solutions
- Helps avoid dismissing an idea before it has had a good think-through
- Opens the door to compromise and understanding other points of view
- Pushes you to see the cause-and-effect relationship resulting from other perspectives

Fear, uncertainty, or doubt may suggest such a question as "What if I fail?" or "What if my idea doesn't work?" Simply remind yourself that there is nothing gained by asking "What if?" about things you have no control over.

Priming and Regaining Curiosity

Katie

Katie Roser

Prop/Set Designer, Walt Disney Imagineering Florida

As a child, you learned by watching and asking questions.

Do we lose curiosity as we grow up, unknowingly nudged out of us by our parents, teachers, or other adults? Or do we squelch it ourselves, fearing the embarrassment or awkwardness of asking questions that feel or sound stupid? Lost curiosity can be regained, and for curious adults it can be primed by following a few simple rules:

Get an attitude! Get confident. When stupid questions are asked confidently, they come across as requests for verification, not evidence of stupidity. If you don't feel confident, stand up straight, speak up, and act that way!

Do your own research. Never believe people who tell you not to bother because they've tried something already. They may be right, but in finding out for yourself, you may be inspired or learn something.

Relax, live, and absorb! Creative people never stop being curious and don't have a nine-to-five attitude. Instead, if they find something that improves them, they fit it into their lives.

Curiosity leads to information, learning, discovery, creativity, solutions and more questions, providing you with at least nine lives' worth of creativity!

Unbuilding Routines

(signatures)

John Polk, Tom Brentnall, Jack Gillett, Joe Gutierrez, Gary Schnuckle, Mk Haley

Image and Effects Team, Walt Disney Imagineering

If you've ever explored the dynamics of things by taking them apart, you were exploring out of pure curiosity and inspiration in an effort to understand, redesign, or make something better.

What happens when you take things apart? You're building your brain's spatial and relationship vocabularies. How things come apart is equally as important as how they go together (although things sometimes go back together differently from how they came apart!).

Take It Apart

Disassemble a familiar object. Observe how it comes apart, its individual parts, and how it goes back together again. For fun, take apart a retractable ballpoint pen. Look at the clicky part, the spring, and the assembly to screw it together. Reassemble it. What did you observe? What made it work? Find any simple household item that you can take apart and explore how it works (with permission where needed!). Perhaps you have an old computer mouse. How does a trackball fit inside the bottom of it? Or check out your toilet: what if you flush it with the top lid off? What happens if you hold the ball assembly in the toilet tank up?

Break It

What happens when something breaks? An opportunity to learn is at your door. Bypass getting upset, embrace your accidents, and consider failure a friend! Break something. Or when you accidentally break something, use it. Pick up the pieces and observe how they go together. If you can't figure out how to reassemble it, consider what you might make it into, then do just that. Embrace the opportunity to learn how things work when something goes wrong, how to fix them, and what their potential is when broken.

Turn negatives into positives to create opportunity.

Curiosity in Action: "Why" Times Nine

Tommy

Tommy Jones
Technical Director, Show/Ride Systems Engineering

If you are interested in pushing the state of the art or the status quo be prepared to enthusiastically ask or answer the question, "Why?"

Asking "Why?" implies curiosity and evokes emotions. When properly responded to, this question becomes the glue that holds high-risk–project teams together. Answering the question "Why?" creates a bond between the persons asking and answering. I have found that this question needs to be asked at least three times to initiate, develop, and complete the bond. When asked "Why?" embrace the question and proudly answer it.

Why?

Use this exercise when developing new ideas, concepts, schedules, or work approaches or when reviewing or assessing work products. Start by giving the tasks your best shot. Then self-analyze by asking the question "Why?" nine times, three times from each of the following three perspectives: leaders, peers, and your subordinates or team members.

For example, in reviewing or assessing a work product, ask, "Why are we doing it this way?" Write out the responses and review them.

The information from this exercise can help inform and persuade those on your project. If you convince your leaders, they will provide resources; convince your peers, and they will help remove obstacles and create synergy with their work; and convince your subordinates or members of your team, and they will passionately work to make the concept a reality.

Asking the question "Why?" gives you an understanding of your product and the confidence to make it work.

Research

Ethan Reed

Show Animator and Designer, Show Animation and Programming

You can never do enough research to create a solid foundation
to build credibility in your work.

As an animator, I've learned that animation depends on the research we do in the development stage. It gives us the opportunity to do in-depth studies of a character's form, movement, physical and personality characteristics, and living environment. With this information we can create believable characters and story environments.

For example, animating a penguin starts with research at the zoo, where the animators pull out their trusty sketchbooks, observing and drawing this miraculous creature. After many zoo trips, drawing the penguin's form and movements becomes comfortable for them. They also analyze video footage of the penguin frame by frame, studying the amazing little quirks of its gait and gestures. The director introduces the personality of the penguin—maybe it's a feisty, young penguin or an old, grumpy penguin. Now the animators begin to draw the thumbnail sketches for the scene and to block out the main storytelling poses to create a believable character.

> **Select a project, such as painting a particular kind of tree. Before you start mixing your paint, research it! Observe the tree in the country, or in parks or neighborhood yards. Study its form and learn about its characteristics from horticultural books. Look at other artists' renderings of that type of tree and observe how they handled the light and how they painted it.**
>
> **Start by drawing small sketches. They are research in themselves and lead to the next step, painting.**

An important benefit of research is that the more you do,
the more confidence you will have.

The boundaries of design are the same as
the problem of perception.
—John Hench

Immersion Into an Environment

Rhonda

Rhonda Counts
Show Producer, Walt Disney Imagineering Florida

*One can be inspired by research as well as
be immersed in it for inspiration.*

How you do research is dependent upon where you are in the process. At Imagineering, we value the story's intent and the importance of being surrounded with or immersed in the story's environment.

As an art director, I found that I was the team member who researched the story by having my surroundings reflect the work we were doing. For instance, while working on the Aladdin show at Magic Kingdom Park at Walt Disney World, I did the research by getting out all my books on Aladdin, researching the elements in the scenes from the film, and displaying samples in my office—rugs, baubles, round lamps. Pictures of Aladdin surrounded me. Everywhere I looked I was reminded of the adventure story we were creating for our Guests. It's my way of living in the story environments we create. At the show openings, I even wear outfits appropriate to the show in order to live the story another way.

> Select a project that you want to immerse yourself in. Make a list of all the elements of the project and find samples (the larger the better) that represent these elements. Find a place in your surroundings to display the samples so you can immerse yourself in them.

For example, if you want to fix up a vintage car, surround yourself with large detailed pictures of its original interior and exterior, very large color samples for its seat cushions, dashboard, etc., and exterior paint job, pictures of various locations you would drive to, and of course, spray the space with new-car scent.

Research leads to inspiration.

Creating a Research Environment

Tony Baxter
Senior Vice President, Creative Development

Research is the foundation for any project that you do. I was influenced by John DeCuir Sr., seven-time Academy Award–winning art director and production designer. DeCuir was frustrated with the lack of interesting images of Siam in the books about Thailand he found when conducting research for the film *The King and I.* He resolved his dilemma by turning for inspiration to the jewelry, fabrics, and tourist wares of the nineteenth century that represented the exuberant story of the country and inspired him to create a unique production design for the film. Surrounded by his magnificent finds, he interpreted their forms as design elements for the film's award-winning production design.

> **Create the environment of your project. Go beyond traditional research and stimulate ideas by locating objects, art, or clothing typical of your project; reading stories; going to museums, exhibits, and movies; and eating food related to your subject. Surround yourself with these elements so that you're inspired by them. You can use this exercise for planning a dream vacation or for services such as catering or party planning.**

Research feeds the imagination's insatiable desire for information that can be stored, recalled, recombined, and used in the formation of ideas.

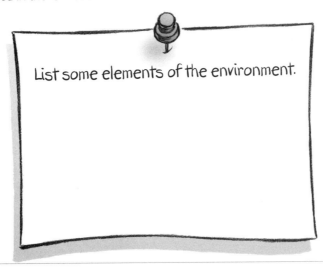

List some elements of the environment.

Seeds of Creation

Peter McGrath

Director, Creative Development, Show Quality Standards at Disneyland Resort Paris Imagineering

Emotion and flexibility are essential when creating on demand.

The first seeds of creation come from emotion that needs expressing and a story that needs telling, but the feeling must be communicated.

In writing poetry, I need to be moved by something or someone. Without communicating the feeling, I can't create anything. In preparing for work as a project manager, I turn to my roots as a poet and seek the story I'm building. I remain flexible and mobile in my approach to the process and challenges.

Creating on demand requires you to stay true to the feeling that you are striving to communicate, such as the feeling of architectural scale, of a sense of place, of a realm of fantasy or vision of the future, or a romantic story. It also requires flexibility in making strategic decisions that affect the future.

For example, I made a strategic decision when I graduated college to be flexible and mobile. To date, I've moved like a vagabond, following every opportunity to create my environment and realize my potential. Flexibility is important on a personal level, too. Dogma breeds extremism, which can't be tolerated in today's working environment. But one can have extreme thoughts and inspirations if they are tempered with flexibility. Some call it compromise; the Dalai Lama calls it "the middle way." It's halfway between nihilism, a doctrine that denies existence, and absolutism, a doctrine of positiveness. This is fertile ground for creative exploration.

> Draw from your creative roots by calling upon your inner poet, artist, musician, or storyteller. List the emotions you like to feel and be around. Find the poems, art, music, stories that express these feelings. Consider your flexibility: list what you will and won't tolerate about these emotions and how they are expressed. Ask yourself: what serves as a boundary? What is a limitation? Respect the boundaries! Apply some flexibility to the limitations.

Naming emotions gives you access to them for creating on demand and helps you stay true and flexible to expressing the story that you need to tell.

Creative Process

Ann Malmlund

Senior Show Producer-Director, Creative Development

If all is going well for you, keep doing what you are doing.

Opportunities definitely come along. It's like dancing with life: you're one-half of the dance, so be light on your feet, keep moving so you can react to the other half as it comes along.

If things are not going as well as you would like or if you need to start the dance, keep reading. Everyone in this book will have a different way of dealing with creative blocks or the problem of getting started on a new project. You just need that first little push. I use the ones I learned from teachers, friends, and coworkers. They remind me of what I already know and have just forgotten.

Inspiration: Watch and talk with people who do what you do (for me that means artists).

Encouragement: Keep working. A college professor told my painting class that when we did a great painting, we'd do the next twenty trying to recreate the initial excitement and success of the first work. Keep going. You'll find it.

Motivation: Go to museums and galleries. I never get over the shock of seeing the artwork I've admired in books in these places. It's always bigger, messier, and more human than I expect. Reproductions give you the image but none of the heat and majesty of the actual work.

Stimulation: Do a lot of different things. They feed each other and exercise your brain. Carving wood, throwing clay pots, sketching, using a computer, gardening, interior decorating, reading books—all wake up the eyes and the imagination.

Passion: Live, love, and laugh. It all shows up in your work, because your work can only be as full and rich as your heart and brain.

Learning: Learn the rules. Then, put them in the back part of your brain, the unconscious part. Work freely; you have the tools. The work should be about feeling and concept, not technique.

Learning from Others

If fear stifles your creativity, work on taking risks and learning from others. You can also call on others when you're stumped on generating ideas or solving a challenge.

Often, the fear of embarrassment stifles creativity because we are afraid of looking foolish in taking a risk. Others times, creativity is stifled because we think it's cheating to employ an expert's style or techniques (even though most experts build their work on the good ideas of others). So why not learn from the experts?

Identify your creative challenge or pick a problem needing a creative solution.

- Who are the current experts in the field/s? Identify and list those who can solve the problem better than you.
- Pretend you're one of the experts. Use their style, panache, and typical behavior to come up with a solution.
- Rough out some features of your expert's solution. Ask yourself: How would the expert proceed differently? How would his or her final product look compared to yours? Write down anything that comes to mind that hallmarks their work.
- Do you see anything that prompts you to take a risk or that you might learn from your experts?

—Bill West
Senior Software Engineer, Scientific Systems, Show/Ride Engineering

DO NOT ERASE!!

Should there not be an expert in the field and you really are stumped for ideas, then you need to go over-the-top with your thinking. If this sounds a little nuts, well, that's exactly the point. In fact, the nuttier you get, the better it works! The object is to access your imaginary creative think tank. For me, it's a motley crew of family members, friends, imaginary characters, even my dogs!

Select the members of your team from those around you—people, pets, characters (even stuffed ones). They do not have to know anything about the challenge you are solving (in fact, it is probably better if they don't), nor do they have to physically show up. They live in your imagination. Dialogue with them mentally or in written form about your challenge. When you're stuck, "ask" your imaginary creative think tank to help out by brainstorming with you! You never know what good ideas will surface.

—Jason Grandt
Graphic Designer
Creative Development

Just Ask

Anne Wheelock
Research Specialist, Information Research Center

If you are stuck, or unsure where to go next with your idea, or need further information, ask someone for help. Asking for more information sparks creativity in directions not previously considered.

My job at Imagineering's research library is to help people find what they need to know or want to see. The principles I use in helping people are:

Start with the intent of finding the requested picture, fact, or style.

Look for things that are related to the request or might be interesting to the requester.

Keep in mind that something I've selected may spark another idea or approach to their concept that is quite different than their original vision.

> **Make a list of everyone you think might have the information you need: a librarian, professor, engineer, or a hobbyist. For some really creative thinking, try asking a child or a teenager. Include the names of all the interesting people that you know or who come to your attention. Note what is interesting about the people on your list and how they are different from you. Form your question or request—it doesn't have to be precise—and decide whom to ask first. Be open to their responses. Their information may inspire you to create amazing things that bear only a vague resemblance to the initial idea.**

The answers you get will help to diversify your thinking and spur creative solutions. You may be surprised with what you get and find yourself creating in an exciting new direction.

Questions stimulate creativity and inform!
—Ginnie Gallo

Surround yourself with visuals and written information from the library and Internet, then start doodling.
—Dave Minichiello

Ideas in a Frame

Doris Hardoon Woodward

Former Senior Show Producer. Currently: Exhibit, Resort, and Graphic Designer

Why has thinking "inside the box" gotten a bum wrap?

I think "inside the box" all the time and it works well for me. I frame my ideas within a box, but my ideas are outside the box. Have I confused you? Ultimately, your design will have a frame or a box around it, whether it's a CD cover design, a company logo, or a gallery painting—each has a frame. This approach keeps my "outside the box" ideas focused on what the final design needs to be.

> **Decide what box your creative project will end up in. If you're redecorating the kitchen, it's the room; if you're painting a picture, it's the canvas; or if you're taking a photograph, the lenses shape the box.**
>
> **Visualize your project in its completed form within its frame. Go for details; see how many you can imagine. Make visual or written notes. Lists with descriptions are great. Refer to your notes and make any changes necessary as you realize your idea.**

Train your brain to go into box or frame mode. Instead of using your fingers to create a box frame around something, like cameramen do in the movies, visualize it in your brain and your inner eye will soon do it automatically.

Visual Skill

Susan (signature)

Susan Zavala
Visual Communications Representative

Visual skills are a part of the imagination's ability to creatively come up with possible solutions.

Creative visualization is an internal sensory process designed to let you see, feel, hear, or sometimes taste ideas and then to test various methods of realizing them in the imagination.

When designing a presentation, it takes visual skill to see all the elements in the mind's eye, organize them, make adjustments, and produce it. My job is to create and design digital presentations that communicate ideas with text and images. The goal is to make the presentation look good and feel good while informing with simple elegance.

For instance, when I am working with plain text, I consider the letters in terms of their overall shapes and the feeling they convey. If a piece of display text is made up of mainly round shapes, I visualize how it might complement similar images and spaces in the presentation. Using this process, I can find the balance and harmony of text and images. Once I see the layout in my head and feel the effect of the images, I mock it up on my computer to see if I am on the right track.

Supplies*: a bouquet of mixed flowers, a glass vase, water, and scissors*

> **Separate the flowers to see the colors and stem lengths clearly. In your mind's eye, arrange the colors and heights based on the feeling you want to create. Slowly put each flower in the vase, paying close attention to the image you have visualized and how you feel.**
> **Listen to what your head and gut tell you about harmony and balance. Cut a stem down a bit if that's what it takes to make the design work.**

Sometimes you get the feeling of what you want before you see it in your imagination, and there are times when you will hear it first.

All the senses work together in creative visualization to help you realize what you want.

Multidimensional Visual Thinking

Rick Rothschild
Senior Vice President, Executive Show Director

Multidimensional visual thinking is an important skill to have for creative work, especially when working with three-dimensional projects.

As a theatrical production designer I put together environments in my head. I use multidimensional thinking to visualize the stage sets and story environments. What I see is not static, however. I can see a space or an object in my mind's eye and much like computer graphics imagery, I can walk through the space or turn the object around in my mind. It's essential to making an idea real.

> Sit comfortably and choose something to look at. Study it carefully. Then close your eyes and recall the images. Keeping your eyes closed, explore the image painted in your mind's eye to the fullest. Try to recall every detail. Open your eyes and look at the image in the real world again. Notice what you missed in your mental picture, and what you invented! Note that the additions are as much a learning experience as the pieces you missed.

The additions indicate the connections or links that your information bank has made with the objects in the real world. The missing pieces indicate what you are editing from the image. Repeat this exercise, removing what has been added and adding what has been edited until the image in your mind's eye matches the one you have been studying. To continue this exercise, notice if the mental image is projected in front of you like a film or if you are included in it. In either case, interact with each of the objects in it by picking one up and putting it back down again. Continue to interact with the image's objects in more complex ways, building your multidimensional thinking skills.

The more ways you learn to think visually, the more ways you have to solve creative problems. In addition, you have more skill in recognizing how others think, which leads to concise communication, a skill important to individual creative success and working in a creative team environment.

Breaking It Down

Nina Rae Vaughn
Senior Show Designer, Concept Design/Creative Division

When working with a great amount of complex visual information, break it down.

I visualize concepts and ideas in paintings at Imagineering. With experimentation and mentoring, I have learned to communicate complex visual information by breaking it down into basic components.

Detail List

Complex visual information is made up of details that relate to the overall composition or project. Break it down by making extensive written lists of each of the visual details. Name each one and describe its characteristics. Then group the details in categories and relate them to the overall composition or project. Now you have a written map for organizing visual images.

Small Sketches

Use 2" x 2" thumbnail sketches (quick line drawings) when organizing complex visual information. Use simple line drawings, stick figures, or symbols—it's all one can do working in this small size. Sketch all the ideas that you need to communicate visually. Do as many sketches as you want; then review, evaluate, and select the ones you know will work best. Now you're ready to work on your painting, composition, or project.

Almost everything we create has a visual component, and we need to use as many visual tools as possible to solve creative challenges.

Doodle space! Any place you can find to put pen to page.
—Steve Beyer

Voice-Overs: Expressed Emotion

Brian Nefsky
Casting Coordinator, Theme Park Productions

Just like an actor on the stage or in the movies, the voice-over actor has to create the role's mood and emotion.

Doing voice-overs may *seem* like the easiest job in show business. You don't have to memorize lines or dress up. You just need a pleasant sounding voice and the ability to read what's on the page.

Being in charge of Imagineering's voice casting for the last ten years has taught me that a really fine voice-over actor creates a character as he or she interprets the lines. The best ones physicalize emotion as a way of visualizing their character and adding excitement to their performance.

> **Start with this deceptively simple sentence:**
> **"The park will close in fifteen minutes."**
> To the naked eye or ear, there isn't much you can do with it. Or is there? Emphasize different words in the sentence to see how it sounds.
>
> The ***park*** will close in fifteen minutes.
>
> The park ***will*** close in fifteen minutes.
>
> The park will ***close*** in fifteen minutes.
>
> The park will close in ***fifteen*** minutes.

Read it again using different emotions: happiness, sadness, fear, goofiness. Use your eyes, mouth, hands, and arms, as well as your voice to fully express yourself. Go for it! Try every emotion that comes to mind. As you practice reading this aloud, you'll see how the intention of the sentence can change based upon which word you emphasize.

Tape record yourself doing this exercise and play it back to hear how you express emotion. You can apply this exercise to any written material you are working with to hear how it sounds.

Give Your Project a Voice

Mike

Mike West

Senior Show Producer-Director, Walt Disney Imagineering Florida

If you are curious about how your project will actually turn out,
let it have a voice to speak. Then listen!

When writing a script or any other piece, I always apply a voice to the words I'm writing. It helps me to imagine how they would sound if read aloud and what kind of emphasis I might place upon each word. This exercise lets me determine whether certain words are conveying the true meaning of what I want to say.

Create a written version of your project or use an existing script or written material.

Give your work a voice. Speak it out loud and see what happens. Listen to your own creative voice—literally. It might be trying to tell you something. The spoken word is very expressive in relating the meaning of a message.

Put an emphasis on a certain syllable, a hand gesture, or a body posture that seems to occur automatically with the use of certain words. How loudly we speak each word or the pitch used to communicate the feeling of a phrase expresses nuances of meaning. Each of these reactions can tell you something about the specific words you choose in your writing.

If verbal emphasis or physical gestures don't help you
communicate your message, maybe you're not saying it the right
way. Try a different approach and give it another voice.

Communication: A Design Factor

James Klepper
Electronics Engineer, Show/Ride Engineering

Communication can take place with a simple diagram.

Technology is a double-edged sword that inspires the creation of things that don't exist, but which can also limit thinking and hinder achievement. The block diagram is a simple tool that Imagineers continually rely upon for guidance in their designs. It helps to communicate the product's basic elements and function.

> **Select a project to diagram. List the key elements. Put the elements in blocks and chart the flow of activity. Think about the communication required between the elements, user, and product. Human beings will want to enjoy the product, so design it with them in mind. Not everything in the first draft will be necessary. Revise it and make it better.**

Here's a block diagram that models a portion of a pizza-cooking microwave.

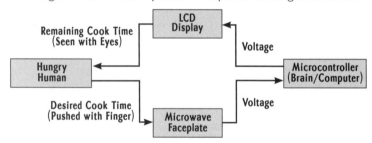

The microwave is an everyday example of the communication between humans and technology. This orchestrated and elegant dance between man and microwave was carefully planned and thought out. The good makers of pizza warmers everywhere imagined what their human patrons might be thinking when they approach a microwave with cold pizza in hand. They agreed that the microwave should do most of the work, while the patron enjoys the results, and that it should be simple to use, welcoming, and not scary or impossible to understand.

The block diagram is a great way of visualizing the communication that takes place when designing and producing a product.

Put yourself into everything you create!

Left-Brained Creativity

Jim Jaskol

Group Leader, Disneyland Ride Control Engineering

When the creative muse isn't around, look for systems and strategies to generate good ideas.

The muses don't whisper as many ideas in my ear as I need, and when they do, they can show a complete disregard for my schedule. I use an analytical or left-brained method for generating ideas that's a systematic strategy for identifying aspects of the creative challenge. It lets me think about the possibilities that would open up if I didn't have to worry about the limiting elements of these aspects. Use it if you like creativity structured and systematic or when you're in a hurry and can't wait for the muse.

> **Consider what you're doing. Ask, "Why am I doing it this way?"**
>
> **Are there agreements with others, such as contracts, internal or customer requirements, directions from the boss, laws and regulations, preconceived notions, current strategies, laws of physics, comfort zones and norms, project goals, early project decisions, or sacred cows to honor?**
>
> **List of all the project's aspects that come to mind. For each one, write several possibilities that would open up if there weren't a limiting element. Look for goals and ideas.**

Pay attention to those aspects that relate to each other—possibilities may open up. Challenge the fixed aspects. For example: design features must be limited in a gizmo to make it profitable. If there were no need for profit, features A, B, and C could be added or costs could be lowered to gain market share.

Find promising goals and alternative ways to achieve the goal. For example, one can forgo profit temporarily to gain market share; search for ways to lower manufacturing costs for a new feature; decide to remove a little-used feature to add a new one.

The real advantage of this method is that you get skilled at understanding the aspects of a project. You understand which ones are flexible and you become more skilled at finding solutions that work around those that are fixed.

Understand the problem, do the research, play hard looking for the potential options, sleep on it, and let your subconscious do the rest. Great solutions make a wonderful breakfast.

—Bobby Brooks, Creative Director
Concept Architecture

When in doubt, reboot!
—Sam Moody
Principal Analyst
New Technology

You can't flip a switch and make somebody else creative, but you can set up an environment in which the switch is more often on.

—Alex Wright
Show Designer,
Walt Disney Imagineering Florida

Some of our tools (methods) are so simple; they work because we stick with them and apply them consistently.

—Luc Mayrand
Concept Designer
Creative Development

I find it important to write my thoughts and ideas in my own handwriting as it internalizes the thought process. Then I start to scribble, underline, and doodle around the words. There is something between the brain and the hand that connects the two, getting the brainstorming juices flowing.

—Don Winton
Vice President, Creative
Walt Disney Imagineering Florida

95

Thumbs, Roughs, and Comps

Ron Collins
Special Services, Creative Development

*Working by hand in the traditional process develops hand, eye,
and brain coordination as well as building problem-solving
capabilities and that all-important sensory vocabulary.*

As a graphic designer, I work with pencils, markers, rulers, French curves, light tables, proportion wheels, burnished type, and—pixels. Keyboards, mice, scanners, monitors, and color printers enable me and my clients to have more choices, but I still work by hand.

Whether the call is for an entire theme park or its print art, an attraction logotype, or the maps Guests use to find their way, I go through an exercise in discovering possibilities and selecting those that will become real. It's a careful and determinate process that proceeds step-by-step, seeking the best solution. You might find it helpful in your work.

> **Explore many possible solutions with thumbnail sketches—"thumbs."
> My college professor told me to do about three hundred thumbs
> for a design. Was he joking? No! The object is to explore a lot and
> quickly. It's an exercise in stream of consciousness; with one solution
> contributing and leading to the next.**
>
> **Make choices from the thumbs and develop these into rough drawings—
> "roughs." Refine the roughs. Select those you'll show to the client—
> "comps." I focus on one clear direction with a range of solutions,
> making it easier for the client to make a selection.**

When the client makes their decision, this is as good as it gets. It's the definitive product of the whole process. And I have the satisfaction of knowing that this process serves me well whether I have the luxury of going through this process step-by-step for hours or just a single hour to come up with a solution.

Ethan REED '05

Playing with Paper Dolls

Tony

Tony Ramiz
Software Engineer, Scientific Systems

If you are a visually oriented person, working with an idea means that you like to see it in your mind's eye before you express it.

As a software engineer at Imagineering, I learned a two-dimensional visualizing technique that's similar to cutting out paper dolls. It helps me to see where vehicles are in relation to each other and to other ride equipment when designing a new ride or solving a problem on an existing ride. First, I picture the physical properties of the ride, the ride vehicles, and the track layout by cutting out the shapes of the vehicles. I make a simple sketch of the track layout on poster board and place the paper vehicles on it, considering the location of ride sensors and the length of the vehicles. Then I can move my paper vehicles around to simulate the ride movement.

Supplies: scissors, pin board, some pins, colored construction paper, and some visual resources such as magazines

Decide on your version of paper dolls. For example, if you want to repaint your car, find a picture of the car in a magazine and cut it out. This becomes your template for cutting the car out in various colored papers to see which you like best.

Or, if you want to rearrange the furniture in your living room, find or cut a piece of paper in the proportional shape of the room and then cut out shapes that represent the furniture (boxes for chairs, circles for round tables, etc.). You can play with the arrangement to find the best design, and it's much easier and more fun than moving the furniture itself all around the room!

There are more advanced simulation tools such as computer programs for this work, but this two-dimensional technique allows visual experimentation and helps free the mind to devise some creative solutions in a quick and inexpensive way. This technique is a precursor to building a mock-up, which would allow you to see the same relationships in three-dimensions focusing on mass, form, and spatial relationships.

Collaboration and Mock-up

Mike

Mike Kilbert

Principal Mechanical Engineer, Ride Mechanical Engineering

*Collaboration and mock-up are powerful tools that work
together in the idea-to-reality process.*

In collaboration, good ideas feed on each other to become great ideas. The mock-up process, where ideas are visualized in the three-dimensional model, sustains collaboration by providing a visual representation of the project for communicating, decision making, and problem solving.

The mock-up works for three-dimensional projects such as a theme park attraction or home remodeling or party planning, where it is important to visualize spatial relationships, mass, and complex details. It is essential if you are working with others who are not accustomed to three-dimensional projects. Start mocking-up your ideas as early as possible in the design process.

Supplies: cardboard, tape, hot glue and glue gun, scissors, and matte knife

Make a simple sketch of your project to determine approximate lengths, heights, and widths needed for your desktop mock-up. Measure and cut your cardboard pieces, then glue them together. Look for and correct flaws that might eat up hours of design or construction time. If appropriate, build a full-scale or actual size mock-up to define details, improve communication with other builders or vendors, and to answer questions about the human factor before moving on to the fabrication process.

*Use simple, quick project models at the essential levels of idea
development or when significant changes are made. If you can
make a model of your project, you have a good chance
of getting it to reality.*

Collaboration of minds equals better solutions.

—Image and Effects Team

Building a Test Track, One PEZ at a Time

Paul

Paul Baker

Ride Guy & Group Leader, Principal Software Engineer

When you have complex creative material for someone to understand, make it easy for them and visualize it in three dimensions.

The more complex an idea, the more sensory information we need to clearly understand it. Three-dimensional visualization, or any physical representation, is a powerful tool for communicating ideas in any discipline.

> **Visualize a complex idea dimensionally to make it perfectly clear and fun. For example, how could you visualize fractions for math students using fruit, perspective for artists using string, or jury selection for lawyers using body language? Think of other scenarios that you could visualize for your complex ideas, list them, and then do it. Evaluate the effectiveness of using something physical to represent the idea versus trying to explain it verbally or in written format.**

For example, I had to send reviewers hundreds of pages of engineering design documents conveying thousands of scenarios portraying high-speed vehicles herded, grouped, and dispersed. These vehicles arrive at Guest loading areas on variable schedules and depart with varying group sizes, merging and diverging tracks where traffic control must be guaranteed to not slow down the operation since eager Guests are in line!

To help the reviewers visualize the scenarios, I added a little PEZ care package to each packet (including a dispenser with plenty of refills). In addition, I sent them a track layout scaled so that the approximate dimensions of a vehicle was the size of a PEZ. With these physical devices, reviewers could better visualize and test the planned coordination of the vehicles by moving their tasty little surrogates around the track layout. And if they need a little "sugar rush," there were plenty of vehicles to spare!

Painting the picture of the world you're creating asks you to think and communicate simply and clearly.

—Rick Rothschild

A 3-D model puts everyone on the same page. It's easier to collaborate.

—Steve Kawamura

Finishing Touches

Susan

Susan Dain

Principal Production Show Designer, Creative Development

Creativity involves everything you know, what you make up out of thin air, and how you apply information, skill, and talent to what you are doing. It will take all of this and ask you to use it differently to produce those perfect finishing touches that make a magical product.

> **Know your end result. It could be an image, feeling, or metaphor.
> Do research to that end. Find a visual direction that matches the result
> you want. Think about how you are going to create your end result.
> Ask yourself: what do I already know that is applicable?
> What might I have to do differently?
> Theorize and test your theories on samples until you get one that works,
> then apply it with enthusiasm.**

For example, I was asked by the design team for Mission: SPACE at *Epcot®* to design a paint finish for the twelve-foot sphere that represents the planet Jupiter in the courtyard. The art director wanted a stylized version that would feel like the real Jupiter and not like a planetarium replica. As I researched photos of Jupiter, I discovered that the visual quality of the colored gases on the planet's surface reminded me of marbleized endpapers from old books, with their intermingled colors that seemed to swirl around. I thought about how to accomplish this same look on a very large and round object. I wondered if the sphere could be rotated and angled so that I could use the same marbleized painting technique that had been used on a flat horizontal surface. If I could control the position and angle of the surface, I could control the direction of the paint as it started to blend together by doing one small section at a time, letting it dry, and then changing the position to continue. I tested my theory, and it worked.

*When you are faced with doing a finishing touch, relate it to
something that you know. For example, how would you paint a
room that should "feel like the look on a child's face when they
receive their first puppy?" You would paint it very differently
than if you were simply asked to paint a room.*

The Finishing Touch!

Making Habits

What consistently triggers creative action for you? Is it sitting in the black leather executive chair and turning on a Beatles CD, or putting on your favorite (and tattered) "Swampwater Beer" T-shirt and unwrapping a grape lollipop?

Is it time-related in that you write or draw one hour a day—same time every day—or is it a place such as the basement, the bathroom, or the garage where the words or images flow with ease? Pavlov had it right—we respond consistently when we are conditioned to a consistent routine. To create routines, spend dedicated time in them on a regular basis. Set the intention that once you sit in the black leather chair and open the lollipop wrapper, your mind and body will kick into creative action, regardless of how inspired you feel or how much creative energy you have for the task at hand.

— Jody Revenson
Editor, Disney Editions

As part of your creative environment, habits offer a safe haven from daily pressures where ideas can surface or they can kick-start creative activity by signaling your muse or brain that it is now "creating" time.

Some habits form by repeating an action three times; others take thirty days or more. In either case, it is important to create habits that will serve your creativity well.

Ann Ching Pynchon
Communications Specialist
Human Resources

Give yourself permission to create a special place where you feel relaxed, refreshed, and receptive to reinvigoration. Include anything that will help prepare your mind, body, and spirit for the artistic and creative challenges to come (or the ones that you face every day). This place can be a physical place that already exists, one that you design for yourself, or that you create in your imagination. It is a place that you will go on a regular basis to enjoy or indulge yourself, let go of worries, where nothing is planned, ideas surface on their own, and you reap the benefits of the frequent time-outs you take.

— Jason Surrell
Show Writer, Walt Disney Imagineering Florida

Creating routines for imagining ideas and executing them is important for your development as a creative talent.
—Ginnie Gallo

Breaking Habits

Dane Stone
Technical Director, Show Ride Engineering

Breaking habits lets us short-circuit a routine or an automatic performance or response, alerting our cognitive and sensory systems that something different is needed. This is desirable for creative activity of all kinds.

These techniques and exercises are not limited to artistic creativity. Engineers, accountants, lawyers, and administrators must be creative to produce something original from available materials, so these techniques can be applied to all disciplines encountering the need for a creative solution.

> **At work, break habits to concentrate on something new or different. List your work habits and devise ways of breaking them. For example, park in other places than your usual spot; find a new place to get your morning cup of coffee or change to tea; sit in different places at the table for the regular meetings; eat lunch with a variety of people not just the usual gang; or call your meetings in a various locations, not necessarily your office. Observe your reactions and those of others. Note how your thinking changed.**

There's irony in seeking creative solutions by breaking habits. Creative ideas like to show up with habitual or routine activities, such as taking a shower or driving a car. Breaking habits keeps you aware and focused so that you are prepared to recognize an idea in unexpected circumstances.

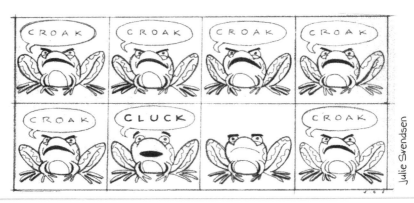

Julie Svendsen

A Left Turn on Creative Avenue

Dave Durham and Dave Crawford

Director, Concept Integration, Creative Development; Principal Mechanical Engineer, Show/Ride Engineering

Many daily habits contribute to the way we think and act creatively.

Familiar routines provide us with some measure of stability, predictability, and comfort. Whether it's the sandwich we always order or the same route we use to drive to and from the store, we tend to be creatures of habit.

The established routes are there for a reason. They are the most traveled paths, and you can get between two points quickly, easily, and with very little thought. However, creativity is like taking a completely different road home—one that you're not entirely sure will get you there but that must be explored.

> **Pick a route that you drive several times a week, but shift into explorer mode. Make discovery your objective and expect to see the unexpected. Bring a pen and journal or sketchbook. As you start the drive, take the first turn available and park as soon as possible. Observe your surroundings and pick a scene of interest, then focus on it, describing or sketching it in detail. Continue the drive by taking other turns, parking, observing, and recording in detail what you see. Once you have gotten to your destination, return using your usual route. Notice if you stay in explorer mode or if your automatic pilot switches on.**

Many creative paths are dead ends. You may have found this to be true in this exploring exercise. With creativity, you must explore many different options before finding the one that works. And after you find one that works, you often need to keep exploring because the first solution is rarely the best one.

By becoming a better explorer you'll learn how to explore faster, more easily, and with confidence.

Deadlines as Motivators

Neil Engel

Senior Principal Production Show Designer, Creative Development

Deadlines can motivate the imagination and change your perspective.

We all have to deal with deadlines at work and at home. Whether you are the entertainment committee chief for your child's school, a layout artist for an ad agency, or an Imagineer, deadlines are part of the job. However, no matter how little time you have to do the task, deadlines can be an excellent motivator for your imagination. To change your perspective of a deadline from a pressured impossibility to a real possibility, see it as just another one of the project's objectives that you manage on a daily basis.

> **List the things that you juggle in a day.** For instance, at home you juggle several objectives, such as getting the kids off to school, planning meals, seeing to repairs, and picking up the kids from afterschool activities. It's your imagination which helps you plan and accomplish all of these things with their own deadlines.
>
> **List your motivations.** For example, with family, you want everything done right to benefit them because it's important and rewarding.
>
> **Select a deadline and then "reframe it."** In your imagination, make the project deadline one more objective to juggle. Give it less emotional weight than you usually do and use the clock ticking away as motivation for getting your ideas sorted and put together to achieve the desired results.

There is truth in the adage "work expands to fill the time allotted." More time doesn't always mean a better-inspired project. With too much time, a project can become overworked and lose its spontaneity or direction.

Deadlines can keep your imagination active,
and ideas fresh and flowing.

Shaping and Toning

Simplicity requires more craftsmanship and effort.

—Chris Turner
Principal Concept Designer
Creative Development

Learn techniques to be successful and have the incentive to invent the new.

—Tony Baxter
Senior Vice President
Creative Development

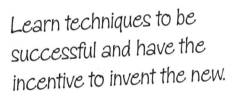

Creativity isn't what's going on inside your head, it's what's going on around it.

—Bob Bronsden
Principal Engineer
Engineering

Drink a lot of coffee and exercise your bladder. The relief will bring on great ideas!

—Ken Salter
Executive Director, Systems Engineering

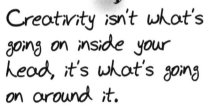

Who Is My Audience?

Bill West

Senior Software Engineer, Scientific Systems, Show/Ride Engineering

Ever consider who you are creating for—yourself, the boss, or others?

Creating for yourself means that when you like the final product, it's done. Creating for bosses and others means working together under constraints such as schedules, budgets, and creative intent to produce a product that will meet the expectations of as many people as possible. It's important to keep the audience in mind above all the interim constraints because it keeps us focused on the big picture, and motivates us to do better and to be more creative. Answer the following questions:

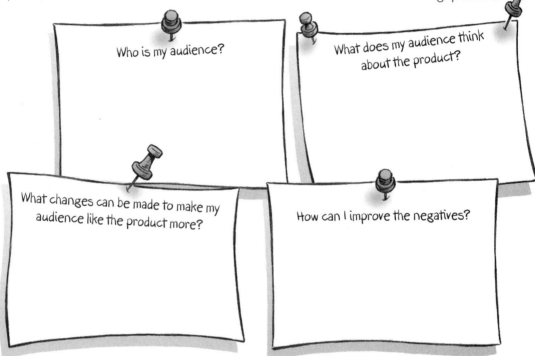

Who is my audience?

What does my audience think about the product?

What changes can be made to make my audience like the product more?

How can I improve the negatives?

Even if you do not have direct contact with your audience, it is important to keep them in mind. For example, Imagineers often have to write documents, draw wiring diagrams, or develop software, and we can think it is being done just for our bosses. But, in reality, we're doing it for our Guests! Considering your audience makes a better product, not only by their standards, but ultimately by yours as well!

Exceeding Expectations

Joni Van Buren

Art Director, WDI Theme Production, Global Retail Store Development

There are two ways you can exceed your audience's expectations.

First, you *meet* their expectations. What you add from there will create experiences that are magical and memorable. Secondly, you *become* one of them, a member of the audience.

Before starting a project I talk to Guests, family members, or diverse groups—people of all ages and types. I ask them questions that reflect my interest in them and give me insight into their thoughts and expectations. Then I consider what it would be like to be one of them and what my expectations might be. I even consider the exceptions, such as what it would be like if I were in a wheelchair or if I were a six-year-old child always looking up at everything and everyone. I imagine what my needs might be if I were a senior citizen or a young mother with little children.

> **Identify your audience or product users. Are they different ages, do they have different personalities and physical types, or do they speak different languages.**
>
> **Make a list of all those you can talk to about your product. Interview them. Let them know that you are interested in their thoughts and expectations.**
>
> **Consider those in your audience or among your product users who are exceptions. For example, are some in wheelchairs? Try to imagine the world from their point of view. What expectations would you have then?**
>
> **Once you have a good feel for the expectations, I try to think of at least three things that would make the project better and more fun!**

If the audience or the product user doesn't have their expectations met, the goal hasn't been achieved. Even if they have enjoyed what was created, they will feel that something was missing.

Changing Perspectives

John Polk, Tom Brentnall, Jack Gillett, Joe Gutierrez, Gary Schnuckle, Mk Haley
Image and Effects Team, Walt Disney Imagineering

*You need a point of view to start with, but how many
can you muster on a single issue?*

Creative solutions can happen when the point of view changes.

Imagineering's Image and Effects Team is responsible for creating illusions essential to the story experiences we build for our Guests. Shifting the point of view (POV) is key to the creating these images and effects.

Habits POV

Observe what happens when a habit has a POV. For example, what happens when you put your shoes on the wrong feet and take a few steps? Do you feel something different (aside from pinched toes)?

Shifting POV

Turn something—anything—upside down and check it out. Look at a picture on its side. Stand on a tabletop and look down. Lie on the floor and look up at the world. Look at things up very, very close then set them down and run across the room, or farther, to see them from far away. Think about the scale of things—what if they were much bigger or much smaller? Write things backward. Write down notes, then cut out the words, toss them on the floor, and see what new combinations of ideas emerge from the scraps. Read right to left instead of left to right.

Change the Rules

Choose a favorite game and change it. For example, what happens if you add another die to Yatzee? What if there are two people who are "It" when you play Tag? Try to play Monopoly in teams. What if you allow words to go forward or backward in Scrabble?

---

*Apply these POV changes to the creative problems you want to
tackle and observe what happens as you change the perspective.*

An Altered World

Tony Baxter
Senior Vice President, Creative Development

Think in terms of the altered world for unique ideas.

Working on Autopia at Disneyland offered a unique opportunity to see the world through the eyes of a car. For example, the car wash became the spa, the repair shop became the hospital, the junkyard became the graveyard, and a fast-food restaurant became the quick-service gas station. All of our visual story decisions were made with this world view in mind. We worked in the same way on "it's a small world," where Guests are invited to see the world through the eyes of a child. The method certainly has proven to be entertaining and successful.

> **Select an object from one of the following: modes of transportation, plants and flowers, furniture in a room, or buildings in the city.**
>
> **Think in terms of how the world looks through the object's eyes.**
>
> **Write a scenario that brings the object or other objects to life by seeing the world through their eyes.**

This exercise is helpful when brainstorming because it encourages our brains to capture what we are observing, and to catalog it, store it, and frame it in a different way.

Wattage

Jan O'Connor
Show Writer, Creative Development

Question: How many Imagineers does it take to change a lightbulb?

Answer: Does it have to be a lightbulb?

This joke brings back memories of when I *did* change a lightbulb into something else while playing theater games designed to free up the imagination, stimulate creativity, and encourage risk-taking.

Transforming the Object

Put together a group of three or more people. Gather and place random objects on a table, such as a can opener, a box of tissues, and an argyle sock. One by one, go and select an object. Each player has fifteen seconds to think about changing it into three unrelated things. Now show the group how you would use the object for these different reasons. If you are not playing with others, you can vary the exercise by writing out three short stories about what the object has become. Transforming the object is terrific for brainstorming a new product.

Imaginary Baseball

Divide the group into two teams, assign positions, determine the batting lineup, and start the game. The ball and bat are imaginary. The pitcher throws, the batter swings, and everybody knows if he fanned the air or hit a line drive. When the shortstop throws to first base, is the runner out? For variety, the group can play imaginary volleyball or doubles tennis. This exercise can help develop any group's team-building skills.

Gibberish

The player tells his or her partner about all the terrible things that happened that day in gibberish. The words should not sound like their real equivalents in English. When finished, the partner repeats the story in English.

The objective is to be imaginative and creative, and to have fun.

Create the magic!

Those Good and Bad Words

Steve Beyer

Senior Concept Designer, Creative Development

Inspired by Richard Lamm

Is the impossible going to the college of your choice, buying the bigger house, or building the next great theme park attraction? These things can happen by creating a foundation for possibilities to occur.

The secret to getting your desired result or achieving the impossible is knowing it is possible. A can-do philosophy clears the way for idea flow, while an enthusiastic attitude is a vital component of a brainstorming session.

> Write a list of words that make creating possible, then put them where you can see them at a glance. Practice using these words in your thinking, especially in those inner dialogues when you mull over ideas. Use the words when writing or discussing your ideas. Practice with friends! Practice making possibility language visual. Keep the words in view during brainstorming sessions—we are apt to forget to use them in the heat of a great idea session.

Words that build energy and confidence allowing ideas to flow are words that make things possible: will, can, like, love, do, make, be, happen, build, bridge.

> Have fun with the negative words! Make your version of a bad word voodoo doll or vampire doll. Remember, energy vampires suck energy out of meetings or idea generation. Pin or tape negative words written on tags directly on the doll. This will build awareness of when you're using them, giving you an opportunity to change to words of possibilities. Change your language, change your outcome. Words commit our energy, help focus attention, and fuel ideas. If we want a certain result, we need to speak the language that will help create it.

There are words that deplete and drain energy; these are the bad words that contribute nothing to a brainstorming session. Some of these words are: try, maybe, might, should, could, sort of, kind of, not sure, but.

List some words that **enhance** your idea flow.

List some words that **discourage** your idea flow.

List some words you want to **add** to
your idea-flow vocabulary.

Lost in Translation

Dave Crawford

Principal Mechanical Engineer, Show/Ride Engineering

If you don't understand what was just said, maybe they weren't speaking your professional language.

I've watched co-workers address a room full of talented people and seen a veil of confusion, frustration, and even boredom descend over the room. When they are talking about roller coasters, it can't be the topic! It's a disconnection in the vocabulary being used.

Professional languages are a window into the mind of those using them and take years of education and experience to develop. For example, engineering "technotalk" and creative "descriptospeak" are two very different professional languages spoken at Imagineering.

> **List the terms used in your professional language that others might not understand, then define them in simple language. For example, "modules of elasticity" becomes "a number that defines a material's ability to stretch under load before it breaks."**
>
> **Write a description of your project in your professional language, then try to describe it in the professional languages of others: technotalk, corporate-ese, or advertising lingo. If you get stuck, ask those fluent in the language to help.**

For example, here is a typical ride vehicle described in Technotalk and Descriptospeak:

Technotalk: The vehicle's body is fabricated from fiber-reinforced plastic (FRP), roughly 10' long x 4' wide x 4' high, and meets color board shape and color requirements. Vehicle capacity comfortably seats and restrains a total of six 95 percent adult Guests in three separate rows. All edges and holes have returns or smooth edges with radii no less than 0.03." All structural steel, drive train, and bogie components are hidden by the FRP body and add-on scenic panels.

Descriptospeak: The body of the vehicle traces the elegant lines of a historic "gangster" car. The surface glows with mystery and menace, while the body communicates high speed designed for skidding out! The two-tone, high-gloss finish lies over the entire body like a dark mirror. The roof's jet black flat finish gives the car a heavy, sinister look, accentuating the bullet holes littering its side.

Surprise! Things Can Bug You!

Anne Tryba
Principal Graphics Designer

Inspired by Eileen Xie, Senior Graphic Designer

Did a lesson learned come your way unexpectedly?

Quick thinking is often creative problem solving at its best. Although minimized with thorough design practices, the production phase of any project can produce its own challenges.

Signage is a graphic-design responsibility, and we designed many signs for the Safari Village area of Disney's Animal Kingdom Park. The designs had intricate three-dimensional and bas-relief carved animal motifs. We decided to have them carved in Bali by artisans who could capture the nuances of the hand-carved style appropriate for this land. The raw wood signs were shipped to the Central Shop at Walt Disney World for the final application of colors and detail painting. After the initial base colors had been applied, no matter how carefully prepared the wood's surface, the paint formed tiny bubbles and didn't dry smoothly. We assumed the paint was the culprit, but in testing it, the paint was found to be tried and true. With a few quick, calm expert consultations, the answer came back: Bali bugs! The curing of the wood hadn't eliminated all its tiniest inner residents. The carved pieces then became the originals used in casting the molds for the signs— mystery bugs and headaches were coolly eliminated!

> **Determine your tolerance for surprises by scaling your reaction to change from one to ten. If you stay calm under fire, give yourself a ten. If you lose it with a few interruptions give yourself a five (then slow down and take a deep breath). And if you stomp out over nothing, give yourself a one (then get some rest and start over with a *really* deep breath). The object is to stay calm under fire using crisis energy to feed your stamina.**

Situations arise in the production phase of any project requiring flexible, quick creative thinking. Learning to be comfortable with a certain amount of chaos or calamity helps prepare you for such occasions.

Two maxims that always travel together:
(1) In the end, everything will work out wonderfully.
(2) Along the way, everything that can go wrong, will.
— Bruce Gordon, Project Director, Creative Development

Know What You Want

Tony Baxter
Senior Vice President, Creative Development

Indecisiveness can cost you what you want. Knowing your role plus what you want equals a cost effective and successful project.

There are many roles that one can have: designer or builder, storyteller or audience, composer or player, inventor or user, and many others surrounding these. You can do one or several of them; being clear about your role and its responsibilities gives others the opportunity to be clear about theirs as well.

> **In moving from concept to reality, roles change. Ask, What is my role or roles? How clear am I on my responsibilities? Write down your answers. Read and verify them often.**

Knowing what you want is the other half of this equation. With each role comes the opportunity to be specific about decisions and needs.

For example, an experience I had on a home-remodeling project really illustrates how the equation works. I was clear on my role as the designer and produced sketches and a small, handmade model depicting what I wanted. I researched the finish materials and indicated them on the sketches. When I met with the contractor for an estimate, he indicated that he would discount his costs because I knew exactly what I wanted. The discount was considerable, and other costs were saved because there were no change orders once the work was started. The contractor told me that most of his clients have vague, sweeping notions as to what they want. As a result, costs go up because changes are made during construction.

> **Make lists, sketches, and models of exactly what you want; research and discuss them with those who can advise you or help you make your decisions. Being confident in your choices is essential in everything that you do (from landscaping to laying tile on your floor).**

Being prepared leads to confidence in decision making. It is simple to do, but a step that many do not take.

Diverse Thinking Styles

Steve Beyer and Joe Warren

Senior Concept Designer, Creative Development; Principal Concept Designer, Walt Disney Imagineering Florida

Inspired by Gae Boyd Walters

The potential for a creative solution soars with diverse thinking.

A creative meeting cast for diversity has members whose thinking styles, work and life experience, education, and communication styles are vastly different. These differences are notably between external and internal thinkers.

External-Thinking Characteristics: These thinkers are expressive; they talk a lot, freely throw out ideas, ask questions, interrupt themselves (or others) as their thinking changes direction, and form their thoughts as they go. They require an external sounding board for their thoughts or ideas and contribute a lot to the session. People energize and inspire them.

For the external thinker:
- Relax and recognize that you can handle differences in thinking styles.
- Devise a way to capture those ideas you do not have an opportunity to express in the meeting (i.e., note cards, notebook).
- Give others time to think about your ideas and respond to them.
- Find those in the group who will be sounding boards for your ideas.
- Ask questions to illicit participation from others.
- Volunteer to help gather and post ideas in the session.

EXTROVERT

Internal-Thinking Characteristics: Internal thinkers form their thoughts before expressing them. They listen, gather information during meetings, may appear to be uncomfortable in the session, and often express their thoughts after the meeting. With information gathered, questions asked, and things thought through (usually alone in a quiet place), they articulate their thoughts and ideas. Their energy comes from within, and they often like to work alone in places with background noise where the distraction and diversion focuses them on their task.

For the internal thinker:

- Recognize that you can handle differences in thinking styles.
- Ask for the agenda or the topics to be available before the meeting.
- Research the topics and prepare your questions before the meeting.
- Ask questions in the meeting; it is a great way to participate.
- Request that everyone in the session be given an opportunity to respond individually to the topic at hand.
- Request that all members also be allowed to respond to the issues after the meeting.

When thinking-style needs are expressed in a reasonable way, everyone benefits. People learn from one another and meet the session's objectives.

INTROVERT

Project Confidence

Tim Delaney

Vice President, Executive Designer, Concept Development

*Instinct and thoroughness will help your ideas and projects
reflect confidence.*

During any stage of a project you need to go with your instincts. However, there is no substitute for thinking things through; it's an exercise that tests ideas and solutions. Doing smart thinking up front and testing ideas early creates confidence.

Ask yourself
What do we absolutely need? Get these things in place first. Then begin the testing process. Testing ideas is as much a part of the creative process as having the ideas. This process tells you where adjustments are needed or what needs to be or can be added.

Ask yourself
At what point does tradition equal stagnation? At what point do we need to do something differently, and why? Do we have the innovative thinkers to get the project through development and into production?

Note that each of these phases has distinct characteristic needs that require both routine and innovative approaches. These needs constrain the concept at every stage, from model to full-size mock-ups, to actual construction. It takes courage to talk a project through this process.

Ask yourself, what decisions have to be made? What rules may have to bend? What might be the never-ending exploration of possibilities required with every challenge? All this takes confidence, too.

*The more you practice, learn, and make discoveries,
the more confident you will be!*

*Design is subjective and needs to be discussed with paper and pen in hand.
Doodles are very effective in communicating a visual concept.*

—Wing Chao

Casting a Creative Team

Bruce Vaughn
Vice President, Research & Development

As project leader, it's your number one goal to get the best person for each and every task that needs to get done.

Casting is one of the most important steps on the path to a successful project, whether you're creating a theme park attraction or accomplishing something at home. Since it isn't always easy to know who's good at what kind of task, you need to rely on more creative methods when casting your team and, fortunately, they do exist. One way is to imagine what kind of animal each person would be based on his or her personality traits.

> Assign each person an animal trait based on their work habits and personality characteristics. For example, a person who prefers to be alone and is a little finicky might be like a cat. A person who thrives on working in groups and responds enthusiastically to both praise and rewards might be like a dog. Using assigned traits, imagine which type of animal would be best for the tasks.

For example, a tortoise is steady and determined but slow and may be perfect for more tedious jobs requiring patience and attention to detail. Cheetahs are typically good for jobs requiring short bursts of high speed and energy. Let the owl help you make wise decisions, but don't put the rhinoceroses to work until you've decided in which direction you want them to go.

Rhinos are very difficult to stop once they get going!

Overwhelm the problem with a lot of people hours and perspectives. For me, creativity is less a magical process than a statistical one; the more ways you look at a problem, the more likely you are to find an interesting solution.

After years of practice of trial and error, looking for a good idea hiding in a pile of not so good ones, I say seek out the unique and just barely achievable.

—Joe Garlington
Vice President, Executive Producer
Interactive Projects

There is nothing new under the sun, just how things are applied and used. This concept brings comfort that the answer is out there! Expect it!

—Charita Carter, Finance Manager
Creative Development
Divisional Finance

If someone is having difficulty listening to the ideas of others because they have a high need to be right, acknowledge their need to be right by telling them what they are right about. Use an affirming phrase like "I see your point..." and emphasize the strength of their idea. This usually puts the individual at ease, because their idea has been heard and they will now be open to hearing the suggestions of others.

—Wing Chao

Dealing with a Full Page

Mike Morris
Vice President of Design & Production

Consider stepping away from your project to energize it.

Equal to the creative challenge of dealing with the blank sheet of paper is dealing with the full page. Creative pressure increases as concepts approach realization. These pressures come with challenges of their own: time is of the essence; people can see the end result and tend to make changes accordingly; budget constraints tend to be greater than at other phases.

The creative process can be energized by selective avoidance. That means stepping away for a time and engaging in other activities that give the mind time to make new connections. I step away with hobbies that involve creative challenges; one is building things, another writing.

> Do this exercise when you're building something. Step away from it. This is most productive when you distract yourself by doing something that enforces process, such as mowing the lawn or doing dishes, or, best of all, doing several crossword puzzles. Building things requires patience. These alternate activities slow down your pace, making you more patient—or maybe tiring you out and relaxing you.

When I need writing ideas, I read . . . something . . . anything other than what I am doing. I read challenging and unique writers such as James Joyce and Thomas Pynchon, two of my favorites. A few paragraphs of those geniuses and I begin to think what I'm trying to do can't be that hard. Or you can read the work of someone you don't like. You'll realize how you like your own work much more!

> Consider how you might step away from your project's development and production phases to gain a fresh perspective. What hobbies, activities, or interests might help you gain new insights or keep your mind distracted long enough for a solution to develop? Might there be another project that you could work on while your ideas are cooking?

Dealing with a full page of requirements is the challenge of producing any creative project. A plan for handling your full page is both people and project smart.

Going Back to the Drawing Board

Tom Leach
Sr. Audio/Video Engineer, Audio Engineering

With a nod to Marla Hofstee, Manager, D&P Planning and Control

How often do you end up back at the drawing board?

Is Plan B a habit or a desperate scramble for something that will work? Consider it all part of the process.

Going back to the drawing board can feel as though you forgot to ask for directions, especially when enthusiasm is running high. Welcome a return to the drawing board as an exciting new opportunity and don't get stuck on a particular solution or technology.

> Make a list of what sends you back to the drawing board: pressures of due dates, rushing to a conclusion, accepting your first solution to a problem, etc.
>
> Look for solutions and try those that are offered. You will more than likely learn something and eventually work your way to the best solution.
>
> Talk things over with your coworkers during any phase of the work; stopping them in the halls or on the way to lunch will keep you actively visualizing and realizing your solution.
>
> Visualize the project with models, mock-ups, or the real article.

Always have a Plan B. You never know what will happen to your preferred idea. If it doesn't work, take what you have learned and apply it to Plan B. It is a great next starting place.

Sometimes teamwork is like asking a group of Imagineers to drive a bus across the country. They all want to drive. They all know the best way to get there and how fast to go. But no one asks for directions.

—Marla Hofstee
Manager
D&P Planning & Control

What's scarier than a blank piece of paper? A blank piece of paper with an hourglass holding it down.

—Dave Yanchar
Senior Project Manager
Tokyo Disneyland Resort

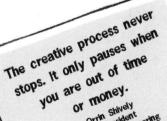

The creative process never stops. It only pauses when you are out of time or money.

—Orrin Shively
Vice President
Walt Disney Imagineering
Research & Development, Inc.

Equal to the creative challenge of dealing with the blank sheet of paper is creatively dealing with the full one.

—Mike Morris
Vice President
Design & Production

Going the Distance

The past has already happened.
The present is what we're dealing with.
The only part of history that we can change
is the future.

—Luc Mayrand

Keep It Simple!

Joe Carter

Senior Software Engineer, Scientific Systems, Show/Ride Engineering

Go for the simple creative solution—it's the best.

Multifaceted, complex, and tricky creations may impress peers, but when the rubber hits the road, it's the simple solutions that are elegant. Simplicity is especially appreciated as a project nears completion because it is cost-effective in materials, time, and labor. Simple designs in most fields are the most dramatic and memorable. Even complex electronic and software systems are at their best when their user interface—the part that the audience sees—is simple and easy to access.

There are many ways to learn how to simplify things effectively. When faced with having to simplify things, I like to practice with word exercises. For example:

If I get paid today, then I'll leave the office, drive towards home, and on the way I'll stop at the bank and deposit my check. But if it's a Tuesday payday, then I'll pick up pizza on the way home. If it's not payday, then I'll leave the office and drive towards home. If it's not payday, and it is Tuesday, then I'll pick up pizza on the way home.

I simplify it to:

> I'll leave the office, and drive towards home.
> If it's payday, then I'll stop at the bank and deposit my check.
> If it's Tuesday, then I'll pick up pizza on the way home.

They say the same thing but the second version is easier to understand.

Consider these statements and simplify them by answering the question: under what condition(s) will I leave early?

> If my boss is not looking and my assignment is done, then I'm leaving early.
> If my boss is looking and my assignment is done, then I'll still stay to look busy.
> If my boss is not looking and my assignment is not done, then I'll still leave early.
> But if my boss is looking and my assignment is not done, then I'll also stay.

Does it matter if my assignment is done, according to the rules above?

Keeping a Bright Idea Bright

Barbara

Barbara Wightman

Principal Show Concept Designer, Creative Development, Disneyland Resort Paris

***If you have ever wondered how your idea became something
other than what you wanted, you were probably in need of story.***

Sometimes you have an idea and you think it's great. Then someone else likes it, too, and with their help it's going to become a reality. You're excited. But as the project goes through its phases there's nothing worse than to watch the original bright idea become dull and something you didn't want.

At Imagineering a wonderful thing happens: ideas are expressed as stories. The team discusses the story to make sure that everyone understands it. In telling the same tale, everyone working on the project makes it richer. They bring their ideas, skills, and creativity to the project. Each individual on the team adds layers and details that make the end result not only as good as the original concept, but better. Story keeps the original idea bright.

Ask yourself the following questions:

What story is your project telling?

How can you or those working on the project (graphic designer, architect, planner, etc.) tell the story using your unique skills and expertise?

What layers and details are necessary for telling the story?

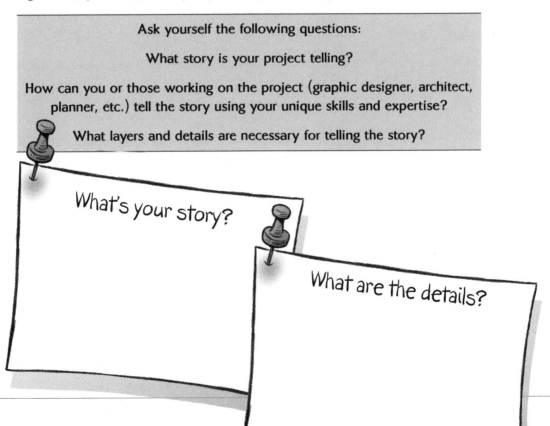

What's your story?

What are the details?

Choose Optimism

GARY

Gary Landrum

Associate Show Producer, Show Awareness, Walt Disney Imagineering Florida

Attitude, specifically an optimistic, can-do attitude, gets you started and keeps you going when the going gets tough.

A cornerstone of Disney storytelling is consistent optimism about our products and people. John Hench, Disney Legend and revered Imagineering designer, often told us that Walt Disney was an incurable optimist; he imparted to team members an infectious optimism igniting their passion for the project.

> Collect stories about people whose success can fuel yours. Record the stories in a dedicated journal (they will become a reference for you on days when you need to be encouraged to choose optimism). Include in your stories how the person's infectious optimism ignites your passion and what you can learn from them. Consider how you can apply optimism to a current project and how it might affect the project's outcome and those working with you on the project.

Optimism and its counterpoint, pessimism, are both habitual and learned behaviors. Optimism can be found where there is a committed intention to accomplish a goal.

Optimism gets us started and through the hard times, where fear, pessimism, doubt, or lack of self-confidence might derail our goal.

Whose success fuels your optimism?

Optimism: Keeping the Door of Possibility Open

Jason Grandt
Graphic Designer, Creative Development

*The door of possibility can be slammed shut in your face
during any phase of a project.*

When the door shuts, it's all too easy to get caught in a whirlwind of negative, self-defeating thoughts. At this point, you need to blow the door off its hinges.

I blow the shut door off its hinges by thinking about people who never let the door shut in the first place, such as my grandfather. He was a drill sergeant, a boxer, a stock-car racer, a chief of police, a master carpenter, and one heck of a fisherman. My grandfather never stopped himself, never let his fear control him, and turned his door of opportunity into a turnstile.

Identify a slammed-door experience such as your project budget has been severely cut or your project money has run out, the materials you need are no longer available, or your proposal was not accepted. Think of those who have never let the door slam in their faces. Ask, what did they do? How optimistic were they? Then ask, what do I need to do? What information do I need? Who can help me? Your objective is to avoid whirlwinds of negative, self-defeating thoughts that will further diminish your possibilities.

Optimism can remove obstacles that we believe are defeating us.

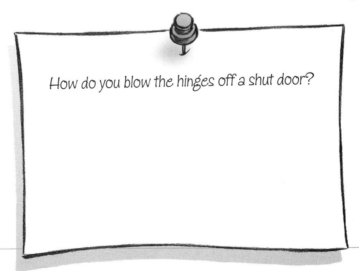

How do you blow the hinges off a shut door?

Hitting the Proverbial Brick Wall

Chris Rose

Electronics Engineer, Electronic Engineering

---

*When stuck in a creative dead end, the objective is to get back
on track and start the creative juices flowing again. Go back to
the original problem with a fresh perspective.*

Preparation: Pinch your nose closed, you'll be digging in the garbage.
Latex gloves will also come in handy.

At random, pull out five objects from the trash can.

**Ask yourself: what can be made from these objects?
Can they be assembled to make a dog, a car, or perhaps
a bust of the president?
How many ways can they be arranged?**

This exercise completely changes your focus. By applying your creative energies to a
random creative problem, you are distracted from the frustrating (and painful) problem you are
trying to solve.

*If the juices aren't flowing, try it again. Use five items you find
in your car glove box, desk drawer, or first-aid kit. Keep it
random! Keep it fun! Include your spouse or kids in the activity.*

Items: *What can they make?*

Writer's Block

Steve Kawamura

Steve Kawamura
Manager, Communications

***When faced with the pressures of deadlines or time issues of
your own, you can't risk writer's block.***

While the adrenaline rush of an impending deadline can be a powerful force, the best ideas blossom when they've had time to gestate, ripen, ferment, and simmer and are bounced off other people.

In the communications department, we spend a considerable amount of time writing, and on occasion, it can be hard to start or keep the ball rolling. It is important to manage our writing blocks.

> **Get something down on paper first. Resist letting the negative space torment you. You need to have something—*anything*—to work with.**
>
> **Put it aside for the rest of the day or week (or even for only a few minutes) and do something else.**
>
> **Then come back to the piece to edit or improve the work, or ask someone else's opinion.**
>
> **If you need to, start over with a new idea.**

You've physically begun the process, and you have something to work from. Your subconscious can work wonders when you have the time to mull over what you've begun. It provides surprising flashes of inspiration while you're engaged in other activities, whether it's doing other work, watching a movie, or reading a magazine.

Success is determined by how much paper you have wadded up and tossed in the corner. List the number of starts, approaches, or strategies you tried before your project was underway. How successful were you?

—Jim Heffron
Senior Concept Architect

135

Nothing is ever a failure. It's true that one person's failure may be another's success. As a lighting-effects designer, I discovered an odd way of changing the colors of an object. However, it worked only under the lousy yellow night-lighting in parking lots. When I showed the effect, everyone said it looked terrible under the lousy yellow night-lighting in parking lots. So I stopped selling the idea. Later, Leonard Yee, a friend and special effects designer, told me about his need for a color-changing effect that had to work under the yellow night-lights in parking lots. Suddenly, my experiment's failure became the possible solution to his problem. You never know when a failure will come back in a different "light."

Write your own or collect stories about one person's failure becoming another's success.

—Mark Huber
Technical Producer, WDI Research & Development

Failures are only solutions to other, as yet unknown, challenges.

Go through all the notes you saved for ideas you haven't yet realized or projects you've put to the side in frustration. How many seem possible to you now that you agree that nothing is impossible?

—Jody Revenson, Wannabe Imagineer

When I want to know if a show is a success, I go to our irreplaceable Disney fan base. If you hit a home run, they will sing your praises. If you produced a dud or flop, they will tell you what they don't like.

Put your project out for others to see: hang it on a wall. Post it on the Internet. Ask people what they think. Listen for constructive criticism that will take your creative work over the top. If it's negative, you have the opportunity to re-think and try again.

—Ethan Reed
Show Animator and Designer
Show Animation & Programming

Success equals motivation. When motivated, I draw on passion, creativity, inspiration, and optimism. The real trick is in getting motivated. I set expectations for success at the beginning of projects and use them to evaluate progress.

Set expectations for success on any project or task before it begins. Measure your progress and completion by these standards.

—Gary Landrum
Associate Show Producer, Show Awareness
Walt Disney Imagineering Florida

Culturally speaking, success and failure are perspectives on performance that have been assigned certain values, rewards, and consequences. In the creative realm, however, success is an outcome that has failure as one of its aspects. Creativity thrives on failure.

Failure is a requirement for success. It goes hand in hand with the creative process. If you're adaptable, failure isn't part of the equation—you just get new challenges when something doesn't work.

Make a list of your project's failures. Look for and list adaptations.

—Patrick Brennan
Director, Show Design
Walt Disney Imagineering Florida

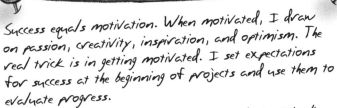

Success is related to circumstances. If you remodel a room in your house, success comes when people are living and working in the space.

Evaluate your completed project based on the response of those who will experience it.

—Theron Skees
Show Producer
Disney-MGM Studios

Success isn't measured by selling a script: it's in finishing it.

List the projects you have finished, the ones you need to finish, and the ones you want to finish. Prioritize your lists and start finishing projects.

—Mike West
Senior Show Producer
Walt Disney Imagineering Florida

Start Something, Then Procrastinate

Scot Drake

Principal Concept Designer, Creative Development

What is procrastination? Are you really doing it?

You might actually be rolling an idea over in your mind, thinking about a project in various ways, letting things gel, or simply waiting for the right moment, instead of that dread state of procrastination.

The most important step in any project is to start it. Sound easy? How do you start? Where do you start? What do you start? What does starting involve? But these questions are second to When do I start? The answer is right now!

> **Drop this book and go start something. (No, I'm not kidding.)**

After you've started it, welcome back! Ask yourself: did I establish a goal, define the challenge, and brain-dump (brainstorm) all of my first notions for a solution?

> **Now, kick back and procrastinate! (Never been told that before, have you? Me neither. I've fine-tuned this craft over many years to an art in and of itself.) Spend time with the project in the back of your head.**

Every part of your life influences how you look at problem solving. Input expands and contracts your mind; sensory changes such as time of day, level of stress, distractions, and mood affect your creative thinking positively and negatively.

> **If stuck in a project, take a break, walk outside, talk to a friend—every situation is affecting the project's outcome, even without you knowing it.**

Keep a pen handy. Inspiration will strike. When you see the idea again, your mind will be in a new location and will pick up where it left off or will tell you to start over. This process of idea construction brings together strong creative solutions that hold up over time.

The secret ingredient to this process:
give yourself a deadline and stick to it no matter what.

Procrastination can be a matter of intimidation! If you procrastinate about learning creative skills, you might think you couldn't be as good as a professional. When I think this, I tell myself, Don't be afraid of it—just dive in. Everything takes practice and failure is okay. So what if I fail or something goes wrong? The best thing could happen, too. Most of the time, the worst that happens is, a little paper gets destroyed. So just do it.

—John Mazzella
Show Producer
Creative Development

THE BEST WAY TO
PROCRASTINATE IS
TO WAIT UNTIL THE
LAST MINUTE TO TAKE
ACTION. THEN DO IT
TOMORROW.

—DAVE FISHER

Perhaps procrastination is just the result of a difference in working style. I've learned that there are two kinds of model builders: those who consistently produce work every day and whose progress is readily tracked on the model and those who appear to tinker a lot while nothing seems to get done—surely procrastinators. Then in a flurry of activity, it all gets done!

—Ann Malmlund
Senior Show Producer/Director
Creative Development

The final words on procrastination are "It's done when it's due."
—Scot Drake
Principal Concept Designer
Creative Development

Is it procrastination? We don't procrastinate, we **percolate.**
—Anne Tryba

139

Step Back for Feedback

Bob Zalk
Senior Show Producer-Director, Creative Development

*Do you get so focused on the task of creating that you risk
losing the perspective of intended guests or users? It's time to
step back and get informative feedback that will
energize and nourish your ideas.*

Feedback helps an idea stand all by itself, in spite of all the necessary pains that swirl about during the process of creating. And you, too, will stand next to the idea, for it reflects your effort, talent, patience, dedication, and willpower to birth something unique and special.

When you've lived the creation for months, maybe even years, you know every inch of the big idea. You know the who, what, where, when, and why of just about every aspect of it. But your intended users don't know any of that. They just know what you've put in front of them, and your product is judged by what is presented to them.

> Solicit feedback from your intended audience in some form of play-
> or field-testing or focus group. Their reactions will tell you what they are
> thinking and feeling about your work. Ask lots of questions.
>
> Use this information to limit risk, judge expectations,
> and understand Guest response.
>
> Adjust your product based on the information you have gained.

*Audience testing gives you information as to your project's strengths
and weaknesses in time to make appropriate adjustments.*

Rousing from a Mental Rut

Anne Tryba

Principal Graphic Designer, Building Specialties Design Studio

Advice inspired by Dr. David Bresler

Getting out of a rut requires a list that will rouse and inspire you when applied.

Here are some of my favorite rousing exercises.

Self-Talk: Start a conversation with yourself. Don't mince words. The you that talks back is allowed to be obnoxious, clever, silly, outrageous, profane, prickly, funny, or honest. During the conversation, bits of unforeseen, unrehearsed drama will allow you to re-think a stagnant situation and move on.

Advice: Ask your inner board of directors for advice. These are people you know. They answer back in familiar voices . . . one of them may sound just like your mom.

New Angle: Physically stop whatever you are doing, and force yourself to simply look at the situation, personal relationship, design layout, illustration, thing from another angle. Hold it up to a mirror to see it in reverse, or look at it upside down.

Asking: Consult, connect, consider, and confer with others. Ask trusted team members or others the very simple question, "So what do you think about this?"

Get Out of the Way: In order to keep from getting in your own way when seeking design solutions, have a creative project on the side that you do for your own satisfaction. You will have total control over every aspect of this design problem and design solution. It is a way of keeping an artistic diary, and the creative outlet for your ego.

My Rut-Rousers

Flexibility and the End Result

Gary Powell
Senior Principal Effects Designer, Image & Effects

*Focus on the end result of the work when
you're in need of a fresh start.*

I like to visit a Disney theme park and see Guests' smiles and hear excitement in their voices when I need a fresh start on a project. There is no greater feeling than watching children run through a Park, trying to be first in line for an attraction I helped to design. This feeling energizes my creativity, reminds me to enjoy what I do, and encourages me to put aside life's problems and project constraints.

Consider a project that needs a fresh start: forget about your budget, schedule, or other constraints which are factors of limitation and adopt a flexible attitude.

Picture in your mind the end result you want: sketch a picture or write a descriptive sentence or simple story to help you remember the result you are imaging.

Write down the key items in your mental picture as elements of a workable plan: take it to the extreme. Capture its true creative intent by including everything you want.

If you are working with a team, communicate your idea to the other members with napkin sketches or stick drawings or whatever would show it most effectively. Actively solicit ideas from the group as you would in a brainstorming session. Or get a group of your friends together and present the ideas to them.

Listen and absorb all feedback (remembering to embrace change). Select the fresh idea and further develop it with the suggestions from the team members or other colleagues or friends.

Explore other areas such as soliciting technical support for further development, estimating your budget, balancing the amount of work with the budget, scheduling your project, planning for mechanical or electrical needs, communicating the end result to contractors, and building and installing the project.

*You will know that your fresh idea is good when the project
constraints start to evolve around it.*

Getting to the Real Solution

Mark Huber
Technical Producer, Research & Development

Solving a problem is a matter of process, assumptions, and learning. Applying these elements in discovering the real problem will help discover the best solution.

Our department administrative assistant complained about being cold. Her desk was in the middle of the work area, yet no one around her was experiencing the cold. There was definitely a problem, but what was it? Was it cold at her desk or was she perhaps just more intolerant of temperature changes? When interviewed, she indicated that sometimes it was very cold and others times it wasn't. How do you solve a problem like this?

So early one morning, I stuck a vanilla incense stick on her chair to watch the smoke from it rise. For more than two hours, I watched that darn smoke move straight up into the air. Suddenly, the air conditioner turned on and the smoke turned in the opposite direction heading for the floor. I realized that her desk was right under a Niagara Falls of cold air coming from the air conditioner. We located the vent and diverted the air to a different part of the floor, thus solving the problem.

> **There are many solutions to a problem depending upon how the problem is perceived. In my story, what are some immediate solutions that could have been offered to the department's administrative assistant? How many can you offer? How effective or practical do you think they would be over time?**

Think back to your own problem solving and identify those solutions that you figured out were immediate but were not really solving the problem at hand. What could you have done differently to identify the real issue? What did you learn about problem identification?

You have to figure out the problem in order to think about the solution. This is true at any phase of a project because factors change as the project moves through the process from concept to completion.

Handling Rejection

Eric Merz

Senior Structural Engineer, Environmental Design & Engineering

You know that you were served a heaping portion of rejection when you pitched an idea to someone and were told, "Wow, that's terrific, we love it!" And then you never heard from them again.

Rejection is tough, and moving the idea forward afterwards makes the difference between rejection being an "idea killer" or "resistance training" that makes your concept stronger. The crucial point is to realize that being rejected is not always a one-hundred-percent reflection on the quality of your idea. The trick is to determine what directly related to your idea and how much was externally influenced.

Evaluating the Pitching Experience
- What do you know about those listening to your pitch?
- Do you think they really understood you? Did they seem distracted?
- What is their previous experience with a concept like yours? Is there a negative history that has to be overcome?
- What is their role and motivation? For example, are you proposing huge expenditures to someone whose responsibility is to curb spending?
- Were you able to make an emotional connection with them, and if you did, at what points did it occur? Did they feel a sense of ownership in your idea?
- What were their suggestions? Did you agree?

Handling Rejection
- Imagine you're in the initial pitch meeting of what becomes a very successful product, and the visionary is presenting the idea to you. Think of a kind way of rejecting it. Come up with as many ways as you can to tell Walt Disney, Wilbur Wright, or Thomas Edison that their ideas aren't feasible.
- Take the role of the visionary whose idea has just been rejected. How would you learn from or dismiss this criticism and move the idea forward?
- Pick an idea of your own that has met with resistance. Where is it now? Is it stalled? Who is responsible for stalling it? If the answer to the last question is anyone but you, rethink what your role in the process is and if you can get it moving again.

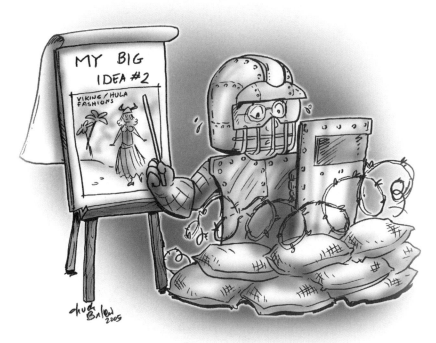

Handling Rejection, the Imagineering Way

Strength Building

TAKE TIME TO RECHARGE!

Sometimes putting yourself in someone else's shoes helps you to come to a different conclusion—to look at a problem from a different perspective.

—Dave Crawford
Principal Mechanical Engineer

The same thing that gives us all the stress in a project is the same thing that will get us through it. Deadlines give us closure with a surge of adrenaline that gathers up all the loose ends and creates an unmatched focus throughout the process.

—Scot Drake
Principal Concept Designer
Creative Development

Don't let your ego drive out your common sense!

—Barry Golding
Principal Technician
Dept 462 Electrical Production

Meditation: daily self-examination on rationality, pride, and productiveness. Choose your actions.

Remember the big payoff! This happy energy refreshes your mind!
—Gary Powell
Senior Principal Effects Designer
Image & Effects

Falling into numb, mindless, repeated cycles over and over again under the banner of managing risk is the suicide mantra.

—Paul Kay Comstock
Director of Landscape Design

Refilling the Well

Jason Surrell

Show Writer, Walt Disney Imagineering Florida

Long hours of dedicated work can cause fatigue,
depleting our creative energy.

Writers and artists need a vast repository of sensory material that they can tap into at a moment's notice: images, sounds, scents, feelings, and physical sensations. Whenever the well is getting low, this repository can be built back up by getting out into the world and experiencing it. Refilling the creative well means saturating yourself with an array of sensory stimuli.

> Make a list of the things that interest or inspire you. Include such things as going to see movies, visiting museums and art galleries, getting back to nature by going for a hike or gardening, traveling whenever and wherever you can, and reading at every opportunity.

> Make a list of unfamiliar things to do that would stimulate you. For example, if you have strong skills in writing, develop your drawing ability, or if you have strong skills as an artist, develop your vocal ability through singing. Doing unfamiliar things puts you in a learning mode that refills the well quickly.

Even the smallest breaks from your work will help fill the well when a deadline is looming, such as looking out the office window, focusing on a beautiful picture, or slipping on the headphones for a quick music fix.

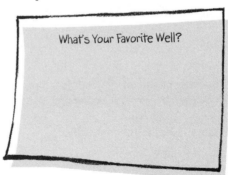

What's Your Favorite Well?

Invent, Re-invent

Jack Gillett and Gary Schnuckle
Principal Special Effects Designer, Imaging & Effects; Principal Effects Designer, Imaging & Effects

Have you invented? It's hard to resist the call to do it again.

If you've invented the wheel, the road is next. For example, the wheel existed for a long time in millstones before man used it for transportation. Why was that? There were no roads. But inevitably, nice flat surfaces were invented, leading to wheeled vehicles.

If your idea is way out, keep going, keep pushing. In doing so, perhaps you'll invent roads for your wheels.

Ideas That Keep Coming
Make a list of your completed projects. Then ask yourself, What ideas
came to me when the project was done? Write them down.
How many of these did I use in other projects? Write your answers
down. Every time a project is completed, collect the ideas that
keep coming in by documenting them in a file or journal.
There is another project waiting for you in the future.

Re-inventing the wheel is a discovery process that builds understanding. Just because it's already been done is no reason not to go through the process. There is a wealth of knowledge to be gained from practical experience. You may come across an alternative or better way to make or use the wheel!

Re-inventing
How many wheels can you re-invent? List them. Pick one.
Ask, How I would do it? What ideas relate to it?
What new advances in technology, materials, or information are helpful?
What can I learn from re-inventing it?

If you don't have a list, think back to the last time someone said, "That won't work! We've tried it already." You can believe them (and do nothing), consider them stuck (and have an attitude), or treat the comment as an invitation to try and see why it didn't work. With your new experience, a little luck, better technology, or new information, it will work!

Creative Renewal: Being a Kid

Tami Garcia

Vice President, Human Resources

No matter how we express our creativity,
we all need creative renewal.

I have administrative responsibilities and need to cleanse my mental palette after a stressful day. There is too much in my head from a full day's work.

For those of us with administrative jobs, play is creative and renewing. Just being silly may be enough to restore our energy after a tough day. Playing with children, singing with a favorite CD, or daring to go it alone with the karaoke machine can revitalize those sagging brain muscles.

Playing silly games with children engages us in storytelling, joy, and fantasy. Story games are especially good because they reinforce storytelling as our preferred means of communication.

> **This game can be played in the car. The object is to create a story by stringing phrases together based on the things the players see. The first player offers a phrase, then the second player offers one, and so forth. For example, if birds, a billboard for Cancun, and an ice cream parlor are seen by the players, the story told in phrases might be: the birds are flying . . . in from Cancun . . . to have ice cream. Create one story after another and notice how much laughter fills the car.**

Letting go and laughing is really important. It is like being a
kid—losing inhibitions and having no fear or judgments. When I
let go of my stress, I am happy; most importantly,
I am the person I want to be.

What Makes You Laugh?

What Makes You Really Laugh?

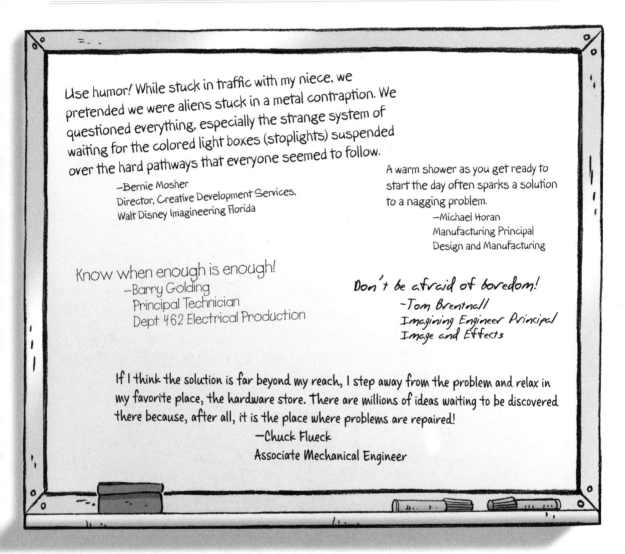

Use humor! While stuck in traffic with my niece, we pretended we were aliens stuck in a metal contraption. We questioned everything, especially the strange system of waiting for the colored light boxes (stoplights) suspended over the hard pathways that everyone seemed to follow.

—Bernie Mosher
Director, Creative Development Services,
Walt Disney Imagineering Florida

A warm shower as you get ready to start the day often sparks a solution to a nagging problem.

—Michael Horan
Manufacturing Principal
Design and Manufacturing

Know when enough is enough!
—Barry Golding
Principal Technician
Dept 462 Electrical Production

Don't be afraid of boredom!
—Tom Brentnall
Imagining Engineer Principal
Image and Effects

If I think the solution is far beyond my reach, I step away from the problem and relax in my favorite place, the hardware store. There are millions of ideas waiting to be discovered there because, after all, it is the place where problems are repaired!
—Chuck Flueck
Associate Mechanical Engineer

Stop thinking about it! Works for me!
—Susan Dain

Box Busters

Scott Hennesy
Senior Writer/Show Adaptation Specialist

Illustrations by Joe Lanzisero, Vice President, Creative Development, Tokyo Disneyland Resort

Have you ever been confronted with a creative challenge where you hear a voice within say, "I'll never come up with an idea for this?" The next time this happens simply say to that voice, "Maybe you won't, but I know other voices that will." Here's why.

Inside us all is Creation—a bustling community of originality. It's a region comprised of upstanding citizens who thrive on receiving downloads and processing that information into new ideas and concepts.

Among Creation's populace are the illuminating Bright Idea; Eureka!, that spontaneous explorer of "Aha!"; and that barometer of brilliance, Brainstorm—each a musing maestro who strives to keep the *create* in Creation.

Unfortunately, Creation also has its share of underachievers. Included among these below-par dullards are the lackluster Namby-Pamby, the ordinary Humdrum, and the insipid Wishy-Washy. An uninspired lot, their only claim to fame has been putting the "ho" in ho-hum.

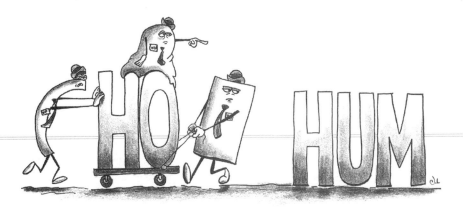

Jealous of originality and innovation, Namby-Pamby, Humdrum, and Wishy-Washy will try any tedious tactic they can to upset the creative process. As individuals, these dimwits have little effect on innovative thinking. When they band together, however, they become bastions of boredom that delight in thwarting Bright Idea, Eureka!, and Brainstorm. What is the most effective strategy used by these dolts of dullness? It's their dreaded Carton of Conformity—a box so insidious that its vacuous interior stifles change, and preventing thoughts from circulating and flourishing into new concepts.

Working in the air of arrogance, Namby-Pamby, Humdrum, and Wishy-Washy seek out Bright Idea, Eureka!, and Brainstorm, and drop the Carton of Conformity on top of them. When snared by this uninspiring trap, Bright Idea goes dark, Eureka!'s tune changes from "Aha!" to "Ah, who cares?," and Brainstorm fizzles into the doldrums.

With the creative flow disrupted, the comrades of the commonplace then use the megaphone of mediocrity to fill your thoughts with announcements like, "There's no way to solve this problem," or "I won't find any answer here," or worst of all, "Why did I think I could be creative?"

DON'T LISTEN TO THEM!

Every citizen of Creation knows that Namby-Pamby, Humdrum, and Wishy-Washy will occasionally employ their idea-extinguishing tactics. So, Bright Idea, Eureka!, and Brainstorm developed a method for you to keep the creative process moving whenever they were smothered by the Carton of Conformity. It is a practice whereby you call upon the Box Busters!

Box Busters exist in all of us. You talk with many of them every day. That's right—Box Busters are the many voices we all have in our heads and the memories of people we've met throughout our lives. They can help you break open the Carton of Conformity by changing your perspective. For instance, you might call upon the voice that is always telling you to go to Hawaii for a vacation. Ask this voice how it might approach your challenge. Imagine this voice tossing out ideas; listen for something that appeals to you (after it says "Aloha!").

Next, change your visual reference and move your eyes to another location. Now recall a person who has influenced, or is influencing your life in some way. Maybe it's your creative Aunt Harriet or your seventh-grade science teacher. See them in your mind and ask how she or he would meet your challenge. Listen to what they have to say.

Now, move to the other side of the room (or take a walk, or even stand on your head!). Just remember to call upon a new voice or person in your mind each time for advice. Have fun! Relax! Be open to different things the voices and memories might bring to mind. Don't give up just because you didn't get a satisfactory answer from the memory of your camp counselor, or your fashion voice that tells you how to dress each day. Simply keep talking to different voices.

Every thought they give you, from the ridiculous to the sublime, is like a saw that cuts a hole in the Carton of Conformity.

Eventually, you'll cut enough holes in the Carton so that Bright Idea will once again illuminate, Eureka! will rip the top off with a thundering "Aha!", and Brainstorm will become a class-five hurricane that blows the rest of the Carton away. Suddenly you will feel inspired and energized, and you will hit upon an answer for your creative challenge. Thanks to the Box Busters, your thinking is no longer confined by narrow and negative thoughts. You are free to explore, build upon, and implement your New Ideas.

Creativity: the Afterglow

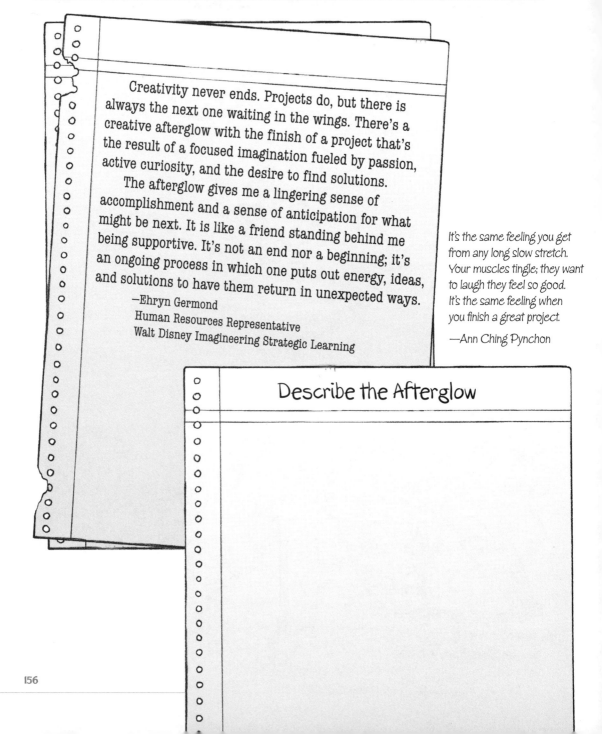

Creativity never ends. Projects do, but there is always the next one waiting in the wings. There's a creative afterglow with the finish of a project that's the result of a focused imagination fueled by passion, active curiosity, and the desire to find solutions.

The afterglow gives me a lingering sense of accomplishment and a sense of anticipation for what might be next. It is like a friend standing behind me being supportive. It's not an end nor a beginning; it's an ongoing process in which one puts out energy, ideas, and solutions to have them return in unexpected ways.

—Ehryn Germond
Human Resources Representative
Walt Disney Imagineering Strategic Learning

It's the same feeling you get from any long slow stretch. Your muscles tingle; they want to laugh they feel so good. It's the same feeling when you finish a great project.

—Ann Ching Pynchon

Describe the Afterglow

Creativity: Doing It Again

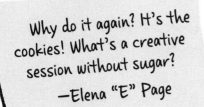

Why do it again? It's the cookies! What's a creative session without sugar?

—Elena "E" Page

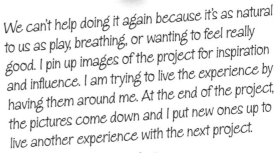

We can't help doing it again because it's as natural to us as play, breathing, or wanting to feel really good. I pin up images of the project for inspiration and influence. I am trying to live the experience by having them around me. At the end of the project, the pictures come down and I put new ones up to live another experience with the next project.

—Alex Wright

When starting a new project, I find the elements that I can fall in love with. I embrace the project, find passion for it, and then I really don't have to think about it. I just do it and then do it again.

—Owen Yoshino

There's really no limit to play.
—Arden Ashley

Creativity is my religion. It's fun!
—Chuck Ballew

Why will I do it again?

Why am I creative?

Acknowledgments

Peggy

Peggy Van Pelt
Editor

I would like to thank all those Imagineers who gave freely of their own time and attended the brainstorming sessions: Pat Bean, Diane Binford, Fintan Burke, Alex Caruthers, Ed Chuchla, Ken Danberry, Anthony J. Driscol, David Hoffman, Tod Mathias, Jodi McLaughlin, Kristi Newton, Steve Spiegel, Joe Tankersly, and Dexter Tanksley.

I would like to extend a special thank you to Marty Sklar, who supported us and participated in making this book a reality.

My deep appreciation goes to the image masters who gave this book its character: Larry Nikolai for Figment, Chuck Ballew, Joe Lanzisero, Ethan Reed, Chris Runco, George Scribner, Julie Svendsen, and Chris Turner.

Thank you to Bruce Gordon for another great book design.

Thank you to Davy Chen from Buena Vista Datacast and Imagineers Brian Kim and Leonard Yee for sharing their thoughts with me.

I express appreciation to those who helped us organize this effort with their knowledge and skills: Alberta Cantreau, Kathryn Fredericks, Sheila Gesher, Max Hamano, Barbara Hastings, Connie Herrera, Sandy Huskins, Aileen Kutaka, Cathleen Nunez, Jan St. Michel, Griselda Trujillo, and Rachel Ybarra.

Thanks to John DeCuir, Jr., production designer, art director, and former Imagineer, for granting us permission to use his father's name, John DeCuir, Sr.

A special thanks to Jody Revenson, editor, for coming up with the idea to do this book and to Wendy Lefkon, editorial director, for her continual support.

Thank you to the Information Services Help Desk Staff, Gail Mitchell, and Herb Ng who solved my computer challenges without fail.

Inspiring Resources

For those who inspired Imagineers and helped them develop creative exercises to shape and tone their creativity muscles we offer special recognition:

David Bresler, Ph.D., President of the Academy for Guided Imagery, former member of the White House Commission on Complementary and Alternative Medicine Policy, and Founder of UCLA Pain Control Unit.

Lucia Capacchione, Ph.D., management consultant and author of *The Power of Your Other Hand* (second edition, Career Press/New Page, 2001).

Richard Lamm, private and corporate coach specializing in creativity and creative language.

Gae Boyd Walters, Millennium consulting principal and Chairman of the Board for the Center of Applications of Psychological Type.

List Your Inspiring Resources: **People**

List Your Inspiring Resources: **Books**

Achieving Creative Balance